STRATEGIES
for Writers
Level G

Authors

Leslie W. Crawford, Ed.D.
Georgia College & State University

Rebecca Bowers Sipe, Ed.D.
Eastern Michigan University

ZB
Zaner-Bloser

Educational Consultants

Barbara Marinak
Reading Supervisor
Mechanicsburg, PA

Catherine C. Thome, Ed.D.
English/Language Arts and Assessment Coordinator
Educational Services Division
Lake County Regional Office of Education
Grayslake, IL

Science Content Reviewer

Michael Grote, Ed.D.
Math and Science Education
Columbus Public Schools
Columbus, OH

Teacher Reviewers

Janice Andrus, Chanhassen, MN
Shannon Basner, Hollis, NY
Teressa D. Bell, Nashville, TN
Victoria B. Casady, Ferguson, MO
Kristin Cashman, Mechanicsburg, PA
Jeanie Denaro, Brooklyn, NY
Susan H. Friedman, Ph.D., Sharon, PA
Katherine Harrington, Mechanicsburg, PA
Dianna L. Hinderer, Ypsilanti, MI

Eleanor Kane, Stow, OH
Jean Kochevar, Minneapolis, MN
Diane L. Nicholson, Pittsburgh, PA
Susan Peery, San Antonio, TX
David Philpot, San Francisco, CA
Jodi Ramos, San Antonio, TX
Jacqueline Sullivan, Sunnyvale, CA
Rita Warden-Short, Brentwood, TN
Roberta M. Wykoff, Stow, OH

Page Design Concepts and Cover Design

Tommaso Design Group

Photo Credits

Models: George C. Anderson Photography

p13, Michael St. Mauer Sheil, CORBIS; p19, Jan Butchofsky-Houser; pp23, 25, 30, Mystery Spot Postcards; p41, useable photos from www.richmondva.org; p89, Phil Schermeistery, CORBIS; p111, The Purcell Team, CORBIS; p117, HINR Photography; p127, Galen Rowell, CORBIS; pp129, 133, Eric and David Hosking, CORBIS; p135, Clive Druette, Papilio, CORBIS; pp140, 141, 143, 145, National Oceanic and Atmospheric Administration; pp155, 173, Joesph Sohm, ChromoSohm; p243, Stephen Webster, Worldwide Hideout, Inc.; p256, Shelley Gazin, CORBIS.

Art Credits

pp33, 34, 35, 46, 56, 57, Charles Shaw; pp83, 116, 118, 125, 149, 176, 189, 228, HB8, HB10, HB11, HB22, HB23, HB46, Marilyn Rodgers Bahney Paselsky; p183, John Sanderson; HB12, Brooke Albrecht.

Literature Permission

p217, Bierer, Donald, Thomas J. Carlson, and Steven R. King. *Shaman Pharmaceuticals: Integrating Indigenous Knowledge, Tropical Medicinal Plants, Modern Science, and Reciprocity into a Novel Drug Discovery Approach* from NetSci's Science Center, May 1996. Permission granted by Donald Bierer.

Production by Marilyn Rodgers Bahney Paselsky

Photo Research and Art Buying by Signature Design

ISBN 0-7367-1237-2

NARRATIVE
writing

EXPOSITORY
writing

DESCRIPTIVE

writing

Descriptive Essay

Prewriting

Drafting

Revising

Editing

Publishing

Observation Report

Prewriting

Drafting

Revising

Editing

Publishing

PERSUASIVE

writing

EXPOSITORY

writing

writing

A JOURNEY BACK IN TIME

by Melanie Van der Hoff

The older people in our family used to talk often about World War II. The years were passing, but the men's memories of fighting to free Europe remained strong. Then the movie *Saving Private Ryan* came out in 1998, and Uncle Harry knew he had to go back to see France again. I was lucky enough to be one of the family members who went with him that year.

The area that our visit would primarily focus on was the Normandy Beaches. About 150 miles to the west of Paris, these beaches were the landing spot in June 1944 for 175,000 British, American, and Canadian forces. They had crossed the English Channel from Britain in boats and planes. Their goal was to retake Europe from Nazi Germany. Uncle Harry was one of the soldiers who made the landing.

The journey back in time began when our plane landed in Paris. This beautiful city became the headquarters for our trip. From a small hotel in the district called the Latin Quarter, it was an easy Metro, or subway, ride to the city's main attractions. We strolled along the Seine River, stood in line for the elevators to the top of the Eiffel Tower, and saw the *Mona Lisa* at the Louvre Museum. But these sights, though impressive, were not the real reason for our trip.

On the fourth day, we rented a car and set out for our true destination. Meandering north through the French countryside, we saw ancient, sleepy villages as well as some with a more modern appearance. Uncle Harry explained that these newer-looking towns had probably been bombed out during the war and then rebuilt. Within a few hours we were approaching the invasion area.

Our guidebooks and maps traced out a quiet route along the coast. From our car, we saw the remains of German artillery in two different areas. The ancient, rusting hulks, once so threatening to the Allied invaders, sat placidly in the sun. We joined the few tourists walking around one site, touching the artillery and looking out to the sea. Uncle Harry did not want to get out of the car, though. He was saving his strength for the two things he had really come to see.

The first of these was the area called Omaha Beach. A long, open stretch of land, this was the main invasion area for the American forces. I recalled the chaotic scenes from *Saving Private Ryan*, the soldiers shouting and dying everywhere, the boats and artillery all around. What a contrast with the quiet scene on the day we visited! Few, if any, signs of the great struggle remained. There was a family camping area nearby, and on the beach lay groups of teenagers sunbathing. I wondered if anyone in their families had ever shared wartime recollections with them. Uncle Harry shook his head almost sorrowfully. "It's all so different now," he whispered.

I wondered if Uncle Harry was ready for the other site he had wanted to visit, the American cemetery overlooking Omaha Beach. One look at his determined face, though, gave us our answer.

The American cemetery is one of the most impressive sites you will ever see. More than 9,000 soldiers killed on invasion day or soon after are buried there. The white crosses, interrupted now and then by Stars of David, are lined up in rows as far as one can see. The simple birth and death dates engraved on the grave markers tell nothing of the agony those soldiers endured. And some graves are not even identified. Engraved on these headstones are the words "Here rests in honored glory A Comrade in Arms known but to God."

Uncle Harry had never given us the particulars, but we knew that several of his close buddies had died on Omaha Beach. Now, we asked him if he wanted to look for any of their graves. Too choked up with emotion to speak, Uncle Harry stood at the memorial in the center of the cemetery and shook his head no. He had done his duty just by going there. And it felt as if, by accompanying him and bearing witness to what he had endured, we had done our duty, too.

Using a Rubric

A rubric is a tool that lists "what counts" for a piece of writing.

How does a rubric work? You assign 1, 2, 3, or 4 points to qualities in a piece of writing to show how well the author dealt with them. The questions on page 10 were used to make this rubric.

" Hi! I'm Tony. I'm learning to write a personal narrative, too. What did you think of the personal narrative you just read? Read this rubric. Start with the questions. Then read the information for each question. We'll use the rubric to evaluate the narrative. "

Audience

How effectively does the writer present the 5 W's *(who, what, when, where, why)* in the introductory or lead paragraph?

Organization

How well does the writer organize events and information that the reader needs to know?

Elaboration

How consistently do the writer's paragraphs have a clear focus and/or a topic sentence with strong supporting details?

Clarification

How well does the writer present details in an order that makes sense?

Conventions & Skills

How well does the writer avoid fragments, run-ons, and sentence punctuation errors?

Score 1 Point	Score 2 Points	Score 3 Points	Score 4 Points
(Novice)	**(Apprentice)**	**(Proficient)**	**(Distinguished)**
The introductory paragraph doesn't provide any of the 5 W's.	One or two of the 5 W's mentioned are in the introductory paragraph.	The introductory paragraph presents three or four of the 5 W's in an interesting way.	The introductory paragraph presents all the 5 W's in a way that creates immediate interest.
Important information is missing or confusing; the paper makes little sense.	Some needed information is included, but ideas are not very well organized.	Most needed information is presented, and in a fairly organized manner.	All needed information is included, at the place where it is most needed.
Paragraphs have no focus or topic sentences, and there are few supporting details.	Some paragraphs have a clear focus or topic sentence, and some contain supporting details.	Many paragraphs have a clear focus or topic sentence and strong supporting details.	Most paragraphs have a clear focus or topic sentence and strong supporting details.
The narrative is told with little attention to the order that things happened.	Some sentences and paragraphs are in a sensible order, but some seem misplaced.	Many sentences and paragraphs are in a sensible order, but one or two ideas seem misplaced.	All sentences and paragraphs are in a sensible and effective order.
Ideas all run together with little or no punctuation.	Some sentences are correct, but there are many fragments and run-ons.	There are a few fragments and run-ons.	There are no fragments or run-ons.

Using a Rubric
to Study the Model

With your classmates, discuss each question on the rubric. Look for sentences and paragraphs in the model that help you answer each question. Then use the rubric to evaluate Melanie Van der Hoff's narrative on each question.

Audience

How effectively does the writer present the 5 W's *(who, what, when, where, why)* in the introductory or lead paragraph?

" Instead of just saying 'I went to France,' the writer uses the 5 W's to set up the background and reasons for the trip. This got me interested right away in how things would turn out. Can you find the 5 W's in this paragraph? "

The older people in our family used to talk often about World War II. The years were passing, but the men's memories of fighting to free Europe remained strong. Then the movie *Saving Private Ryan* came out in 1998, and Uncle Harry knew he had to go back to see France again. I was lucky enough to be one of the family members who went with him that year.

How well does the writer organize events and information that the reader needs to know?

" The writer talks about several places and events I didn't know much about. But she helps me understand by giving information about them—right at the point where I needed to know it. For example, after mentioning the Normandy Beaches, she explains right away why they are important. "

About 150 miles to the west of Paris, these beaches were the landing spot in June 1944 for 175,000 British, American, and Canadian forces. They had crossed the English Channel from Britain in boats and planes. Their goal was to retake Europe from Nazi Germany.

How consistently do the writer's paragraphs have a clear focus and/or a topic sentence with strong supporting details?

" The writer talks about a lot of places in her narrative. Every time she mentions a new one, she has a new paragraph. The writer uses a topic sentence that helps the reader know what the paragraph will be about. "

The American cemetery is one of the most impressive sites you will ever see. More than 9,000 soldiers killed on invasion day or soon after are buried there. The white crosses, interrupted now and then by Stars of David, are lined up in rows as far as one can see. The simple birth and death dates engraved on the grave markers tell nothing of the agony those soldiers endured. And some graves are not even identified. Engraved on these headstones are the words "Here rests in honored glory A Comrade in Arms known but to God."

" The writer follows this pattern in all the paragraphs where she talks about new places. "

Clarification

How well does the writer present details in an order that makes sense?

66 I know that in a narrative you usually tell about events in the order that they happened. This writer starts at the beginning of her trip and moves toward the cemetery visit. Even within her paragraphs, she tells things in the right order. 99

On the fourth day, we rented a car and set out for our true destination. Meandering north through the French countryside, we saw ancient, sleepy villages as well as some with a more modern appearance. Uncle Harry explained that these newer-looking towns had probably been bombed out during the war and then rebuilt. Within a few hours we were approaching the invasion area.

Conventions & Skills

How well does the writer avoid fragments, run-ons, and sentence punctuation errors?

66 The writer doesn't have any spelling or capitalization errors that I can see. I noticed that she avoided run-on sentences— a problem I often have—by combining sentences with conjunctions. Here is one example. 99

Uncle Harry had never given us the particulars, but we knew that several of his close buddies had died on Omaha Beach.

 Now it's my turn to write!

I'm going to write a personal narrative, too. Follow along to see how well I use good writing strategies. I'm going to use the model and also the rubric to help me write better. 99

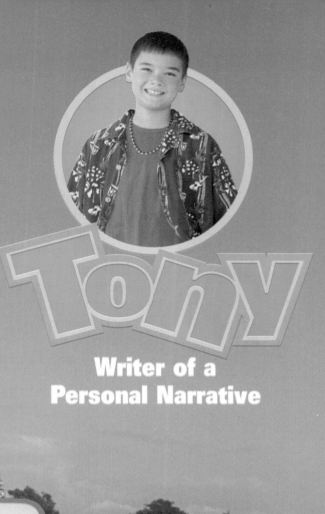

Tony

Writer of a Personal Narrative

Name: Tony

Home: California

Hobbies: swimming, drawing, making up designs for buildings

Favorite Book: *Grand Constructions* by Gian Paolo Ceserani

Favorite Teacher: Mrs. Lewis, my industrial arts teacher

Assignment: personal narrative

Prewriting

Gather
List things my audience should know about my topic.

"There's a great building in my town. It's part of a place called the Mystery Spot. The first time I visited it, I knew right away I wanted to be able to design buildings of my own that were as cool as this.

"When my teacher asked us to write a personal narrative, I thought about the Mystery Spot. My first visit there was really amazing, so I decided to write about it. There are a lot of things I could say, but I wanted to focus on things my audience would want, and need, to know. I made notes listing all the important points. That was my strategy. Here are the notes I came up with."

Notes About the Mystery Spot

- first visited Mystery Spot two years ago with Dad
- a couple of miles from downtown Santa Cruz
- Spot is on a hill, in the redwoods
- stand on 2 x 4s, smaller person looks taller (Dad and a kid)
- board sticking out of window—does the ball roll up?
- floor at 30-degree angle; pendulum easier to push one way than the other
- not really gravity—Dad got the answers
- psychologist from U. of California checked out Mystery Spot
- angles, tilts, and hill create optical illusions (define)
- loved the Mystery Spot, and loved the explanation
- made me want to be a creative builder, too

Go to page 6 in the **Practice** the Strategy **Notebook!**

PreWriting

Organize   Make a 5 W's chart to organize my notes.

" The **Rubric** tells me it's important to organize the information that the audience needs to know. So my strategy was to use a 5 W's chart to make sure I covered all the basics. Besides telling what happened, I knew I also needed to explain why things happened. I made sure I put enough information in that category. "

5 W's Chart

A **5 W's chart** organizes information by asking and answering the following questions: *What* happened? *Who* was there? *Why* did it happen? *When* did it happen? *Where* did it happen?

What happened?

- visited Mystery Spot
- stand on 2 x 4s, smaller person looks taller (Dad and a kid)
- board sticking out of window—does the ball roll up?
- floor at 30-degree angle; pendulum easier to push one way than the other
- Mystery Spot inspired me to want to be a building designer

Who was there?

- Dad and I

Why did it happen?

- not really gravity—Dad got the answers
- psychologist from U. of California checked out Mystery Spot
- angles, tilts, and hill create optical illusions (define)

When did it happen?

- first visited two years ago

Where did it happen?

- on a hill, a couple of miles outside of Santa Cruz, in the redwoods

Go to page 8 in the **Practice** the Strategy **Notebook!**

Drafting

Write
Draft my narrative. Start with a lead paragraph that presents the 5 W's in such an interesting way that the audience will want to read more.

"The **Rubric** tells me to get the audience interested right away. My classmates are my audience. What is a good way to grab their attention? I want to include a little about the 5 W's in my lead paragraph, but I want to make it sound personal. I think I'll focus on how close to home the Mystery Spot is. I know a saying I can use.

"When I draft, I'll concentrate on getting my ideas down. I won't worry about correcting mistakes. I can do that later. "

Lead Paragraph

The **lead paragraph** is the first paragraph in a longer piece of writing. There are several ways that you can develop a lead paragraph.

- **Start with a quote or saying.**

    "The Mystery Spot is really a great place to visit," our neighbor Mrs. Franklin told us. "You'll see a lot of amazing things, and it's only a few miles from here." Dad and I were so impressed that we decided to take her advice. . . .

- **Start with a dramatic fact or event.**

    The Mystery Spot is a place where it seems that gravity has gone haywire. Balls roll uphill, and people look taller or shorter depending on where they stand. My first visit two years ago really amazed and inspired me. . . .

- **Start with a character.**

    My dad is six feet tall, but at the Mystery Spot he was shorter than a nine-year-old boy.

lead paragraph

starts with a saying

A Visit That Inspired Me

I've heard the saying that you can learn everything you need to know in your own backyard. I'm not sure that that's exactly true. I do think you can learn alot of things pretty close to home, though. when I ~~1st~~ first visited the Mystery Spot two years ago, with my dad I was only a few miles from my house. But I learned two important things. One is that buildings can be designed in very intresting ways. The other is that I might want to design some intresting buildings myself. The Mystery Spot is just a few miles from downtown Santa Cruz. In the middle of some redwoods. Dad and I had driven near it thousands of times, but then our nieghbor ~~Mrs. Franklin~~ told us that we should stop there that it was really worth seeing. So one day we decided to make a special trip to the Spot. The signs along the road made it easy to find the place.

ENTRANCE To MYSTERY SPOT

Go to page 10 in the Practice the Strategy Notebook!

Narrative Writing • Personal Narrative

Revising

Elaborate

Check each paragraph for supporting details. Make sure they relate to the topic sentence.

> After I finished my first draft, I read it over. I got a little confused in a paragraph about the cabin's floors and railings. There were a lot of supporting details, but you couldn't tell what main idea or point all these examples supported. I realized I'd better go back and add a topic sentence, and maybe a couple more details, to make the paragraph clearer.

READ TO MYSELF

Topic Sentence, Supporting Details

The **topic sentence** states or contains the main idea of a paragraph. While it is often the first sentence in the paragraph, it may also be positioned in the middle or at the end of the paragraph.

A **supporting detail** is an example, anecdote, or fact that supports a larger idea. The larger idea is stated in the topic sentence.

[2nd DRAFT]

topic sentence

supporting details

The inside of the cabin was just as strange. The floor seemed to be pitched at about a 30-degree angle, it was very hard to walk there. People seemed like they were tilted in all directions and could fall over at any minute, and a few people held on to the railings because they were feeling a little dizzy. An other wierd thing was the Pendulum, which hung from the ceiling. You could push it in both directions, but it was much easier to push it to one side of the cabin than to the other.

Go to page 12 in the Practice ∧ the Strategy Notebook!

Revising

Clarify
Make sure sentences and paragraphs are in the most effective order.

"I thought the paragraphs in my narrative were in a good order when I read it over. They took the reader from the beginning of my visit to the end. In the paragraph about the ball rolling up the board, though, I could see that if I changed the order just a little, things would make more sense."

[3rd DRAFT]

The area where things began to get really bizarre was the cabin. This structure looked old and worn down, but it was filled with surprises. When we walked up to the cabin, ~~the guide rolled a ball down the long board.~~ We saw a long ~~this~~ board sticking out a front window. It was pretty obvious that the end sticking out was higher than the end resting inside. Then the guide rolled a ball down the board. The ball went a little way, but then it stoped and rolled right back up! What was going on here? Could it be that the laws of gravity didn't work in this place?

reordered sentences

Go to page 14 in the **Practice** the Strategy **Notebook!**

Editing

Proofread

Check to see that there are no sentence fragments or run-on sentences.

> Now I need to look for errors in my narrative. I always check for capitalization and spelling errors. But the **Rubric** also tells me to look for fragments and run-ons. I know that I sometimes make these mistakes, especially when I am writing fast. Look on the next page to see how I corrected fragments and run-ons.

Conventions & SKiLLS

Fragments and Run-ons

A **sentence fragment** is a group of words that begins with a capital letter and ends with a period or other end punctuation but does not state a complete thought.

Fragment: A visit to the Mystery Spot.

Correct a sentence fragment in one of these ways.

- **Add a subject, a predicate, or both.**
  Dad and I made a visit to the Mystery Spot.

- **Attach the fragment to a related sentence.**
  Dad and I planned a special trip, a visit to the Mystery Spot.

A **run-on sentence** is two simple sentences that are run together and are not correctly joined by a conjunction or punctuation.

Run-on sentence: I loved the Mystery Spot, I wanted to go back as soon as possible.

Correct a run-on sentence in one of these ways:

- **Combine the sentences with both a comma and a conjunction.**
  I loved the Mystery Spot, **and** I wanted to go back as soon as possible.

- **Combine the sentences with a semicolon.**
  I loved the Mystery Spot; I wanted to go back as soon as possible.

- **Write two separate sentences.**
  I loved the Mystery Spot. I wanted to go back as soon as possible.

Extra Practice
See **Fragments and Run-ons** (pages CS 2-CS 3) in the back of this book.

[4th DRAFT]

A Visit That Inspired Me

I've heard the saying that you can learn everything you need to know in your own backyard. I'm not sure that that's exactly true. I do think you can learn *a lot* (SP) ~~alot~~ of things pretty close to home, though. when I first visited the Mystery Spot two years ago with my dad, I was only a few miles from my house. But I learned two important things. One is that buildings can be designed in very *interesting* (SP) ~~intresting~~ ways. The other is that I might want to design some *interesting* (SP) ~~intresting~~ buildings myself. ⌗ The Mystery Spot is just a few miles from downtown Santa Cruz, *In the middle of some redwoods.* Dad and I had ← **fragment** driven near it thousands of times, but then our *neighbor* (SP) ~~nieghbor~~ told us that we should stop there, that it was really worth seeing. So one day we decided to make a special trip to the Spot. The signs along the road made it easy to find the place.

The Mystery Spot is a pretty small area, *Only about 150 feet in diameter.* ← **fragment** You have to climb a hill to reach it, and the tour guides promise that strange things will start happening the minute you step into it. These guides are not *lying* (SP) ~~lieing~~. For example, one of the first things you see is 2 x 4s that stretch across two pieces of concrete. Our guide asked for volunteers to stand at each end of a 2 x 4. My Dad and a kid several inches shorter volunteered, *and* Then they traded places. It looked like the kid was taller than my dad! I could tell right away that I was going to like this place. ∟ **run-on**

Go to page 15 in the **Practice** *the Strategy* ∧ **Notebook!**

Publishing

Publish my narrative in a class diary.

Writer:	Tony
Assignment:	personal narrative
Topic:	visiting the Mystery Spot
Audience:	classmates
Method of Publication:	class diary
Reason for Choice:	It was an important experience for me. I want my friends to know all about it.

"Everyone was putting papers about their important experiences into our class diary. I thought that my narrative about the Mystery Spot would fit in very well. Here's what I did to get it ready."

1. I checked my narrative one more time to be sure it was as good as I could make it.

2. I found some postcards I bought at the Mystery Spot and pasted them onto construction paper.

3. I punched holes in all the pages so they would fit into a binder.

4. I added my narrative to the class diary.

A Visit That Inspired Me

by Tony

I've heard the saying that you can learn everything you need to know in your own backyard. I'm not sure that that's exactly true. I do think you can learn a lot of things pretty close to home, though. When I first visited the Mystery Spot two years ago with my dad, I was only a few miles from my house. But I learned two important things. One is that buildings can be designed in very interesting ways. The other is that I might want to design some interesting buildings myself.

The Mystery Spot is just a few miles from downtown Santa Cruz, in the middle of some redwoods. Dad and I had driven near it thousands of times, but then our neighbor told us that we should stop there, that it was really worth seeing. So one day we decided to make a special trip to the Spot. The signs along the road made it easy to find the place.

The Mystery Spot is a pretty small area, only about 150 feet in diameter. You have to climb a hill to reach it, and the tour guides promise that strange things will start happening the minute you step into it. These guides are not lying. For example, one of the first things you see is 2 x 4s that stretch across two pieces of concrete. Our guide asked for volunteers to stand at each end of a 2 x 4. My dad and a kid several inches shorter volunteered, and then they traded places. It looked like the kid was taller than my dad! I could tell right away that I was going to like this place.

The area where things began to get really bizarre was the cabin. This structure looked old and worn down, but it was filled with surprises. When we walked up to the cabin, we saw a long board sticking out a front window. It was pretty obvious that the end sticking out was higher than the end resting inside. Then the guide rolled a ball down the board. The ball went a little way, but then it stopped and rolled right back up! What was going on here? Could it be that the laws of gravity didn't work in this place?

Narrative Writing • Personal Narrative

The inside of the cabin was just as strange. The floor seemed to be pitched at about a 30-degree angle, and it was very hard to walk there. People seemed like they were tilted in all directions and could fall over at any minute. Another weird thing was the pendulum, which hung from the ceiling. You could push it in both directions, but it was much easier to push it to one side of the cabin than to the other.

I was finding the Mystery Spot totally fascinating, but I was also wondering what was going on. Our guide kept talking about strange gravitational forces, but my logical mind was telling me that this didn't quite make sense.

A few days later, Dad came home from work with some answers. One of his coworkers told him that a psychologist from the University of California had checked out the place. He discovered that all the strange things we had experienced are based on optical illusions, or sights that appear different from what they really are. Remember that the Mystery Spot was built on a hill. That, along with the crazy angles and tilted walls, confuses people into thinking things are not level—when they actually are.

I loved the Mystery Spot, and after I heard this explanation I loved it even more. It showed me that people could design houses or other buildings to create all sorts of impressions. They aren't exactly optical illusions, but there must be ways to make small rooms seem bigger and tall buildings seem even higher. I thought about some of the drawings I've done in industrial arts class. Maybe I could learn to combine my ideas into plans for some really neat buildings.

USING the Rubric for Assessment

Go to page 16 in the **Practice Notebook!** Use that rubric to assess Tony's paper. Try using the rubric to assess your own writing.

the Strategy

NARRATIVE writing

Historical Fiction Episode

In this chapter, you will have a chance to do one kind of narrative writing, a **historical fiction episode**.

A **historical fiction episode** is a made-up story that uses an actual time, place, and/or characters. Fiction and historical facts are blended together.

The piece of writing on the next three pages is historical fiction. Read these questions. Then read the story. Keep the questions in mind as you read.

 **How well does the writer hold the audience's interest throughout the story?**

 **How clearly does the story flow from beginning to middle to end?**

 **How effectively does the writer use historical details to make the story sound authentic?**

 **How realistic is the dialogue spoken by the characters?**

 **How consistently does the writer use the correct punctuation for quotations?**

Wanted: A Boat to India

by Art Foley

Marco Polo was beginning to wonder if he was ever going to get to Cathay. His father and uncle had returned to Venice from that country in the Far East laden with spices, gold, and other rich treasures. Marco had been excited when the men said he could accompany them on this next trip, but so far things had not gone smoothly. They had traveled far out of their way to avoid a war in Armenia. They had struggled across a vast, hot desert in Persia where packs of bandits roamed around terrorizing travelers. Then the other day their own party had been attacked by one of these bandit hordes, and they had been lucky to escape alive.

Now, though, they were finally at Hormuz, at the edge of the sea.

"It's as hot here as it was in the desert," Marco said to himself. "But maybe our luck will change. Maybe we will be able to hire a boat that will get us at least as far as India."

Marco accompanied Niccolò and Maffeo, his father and uncle, when they went down to the harbor. Along with them went Omar, a trader from Hormuz who had recently done business with them. Omar, a tall man with a broad face and easy smile, assured them that they would have no trouble getting a boat.

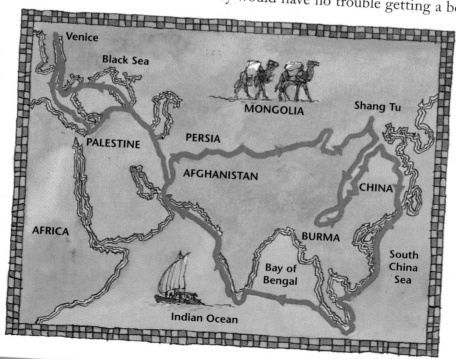

"Look at all the ships in this harbor," he insisted. "These captains and their crews cross back and forth to India every week. They will fall all over themselves trying to get your business."

The Polos looked around a little doubtfully. The harbor was indeed filled with boats. Their crooked triangular sails swayed slightly as a hot breeze rippled through them. All but two or three of the boats, though, looked far too small to make the crossing.

"Talk to that captain over there," Niccolò told Omar, "and ask if we can see his boat."

"An excellent choice," Omar praised him. "This man has been a captain for over twenty years with never a mishap."

Even as they approached the boat, however, the Polos began to get apprehensive. Like all the others, it had only one mast, one rudder, and one sail.

"Ask the captain how his ship can be seaworthy," Maffeo told Omar. "What happens if that single mast snaps in the wind? And what holds the boards together? I don't see any iron nails."

"Of course there aren't any nails," Omar responded. "Shipbuilders around here use wooden pegs, which work quite well. They stitch the planks together with strong threads made of coconut fibers. And the masts are lightweight and very flexible. I think perhaps you are worrying too much."

Maffeo reminded Omar that Venice, the city where the Polos lived, was known for its merchants sailing to distant ports. He and his brother had seen a good ship or two in their day.

"These ships are lightweight and flexible," Omar continued, almost as if he hadn't heard them. "They are well suited to ride the storms of the Indian Ocean."

Marco was getting a little tired of listening to this haggling. These boats don't look so bad to me, he thought. Isn't it important for us to try to move along?

Marco looked up at the boat owner, who was gesturing to him to climb aboard. As soon as he did, a foul odor assailed his nose. "Could you ask the captain what causes that terrible smell?" he called down to Omar.

"It's the fish oil," Omar explained. "Shipbuilders in this region use the oil instead of tar to caulk the seams of the boat. And really, the oil, despite the bad smells, does its job quite well. These ships are lightweight and flexible, and. . . ."

By this time, all the Polos, even Marco, had had enough. They just could not believe that small, flimsy boats like these, held together with wooden pegs and fish oil, could get them safely to their destination. They thanked their friend Omar for his help, nodded politely to the captain, and walked away.

I guess we haven't gotten rid of our bad luck yet, thought Marco. We will have to find another way to continue eastward.

Using a Rubric

A rubric is a tool that tells "what counts" in a piece of writing.

How do you use a rubric? You assign 1, 2, 3, or 4 points to qualities in the writing. These points show how well the author dealt with the various qualities.

The questions on page 32 were used to make this rubric.

"Hi! My name is Quiana. I'm learning about historical fiction episodes, too. What did you think of the story on pages 33–35? Take a look at this rubric. Begin with the questions; then go on to read the scoring information for each question. We'll be using the rubric to evaluate the historical fiction story you just read."

Audience

How well does the writer hold the audience's interest throughout the story?

Organization

How clearly does the story flow from beginning to middle to end?

Elaboration

How effectively does the writer use historical details to make the story sound authentic?

Clarification

How realistic is the dialogue spoken by the characters?

Conventions & Skills

How consistently does the writer use the correct punctuation for quotations?

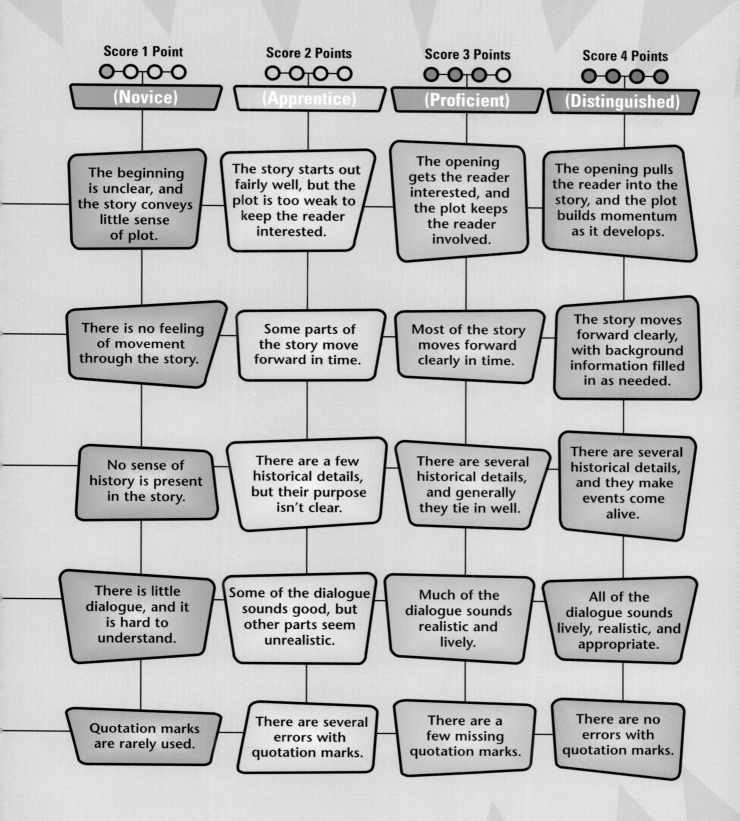

Score 1 Point
(Novice)

The beginning is unclear, and the story conveys little sense of plot.

There is no feeling of movement through the story.

No sense of history is present in the story.

There is little dialogue, and it is hard to understand.

Quotation marks are rarely used.

Score 2 Points
(Apprentice)

The story starts out fairly well, but the plot is too weak to keep the reader interested.

Some parts of the story move forward in time.

There are a few historical details, but their purpose isn't clear.

Some of the dialogue sounds good, but other parts seem unrealistic.

There are several errors with quotation marks.

Score 3 Points
(Proficient)

The opening gets the reader interested, and the plot keeps the reader involved.

Most of the story moves forward clearly in time.

There are several historical details, and generally they tie in well.

Much of the dialogue sounds realistic and lively.

There are a few missing quotation marks.

Score 4 Points
(Distinguished)

The opening pulls the reader into the story, and the plot builds momentum as it develops.

The story moves forward clearly, with background information filled in as needed.

There are several historical details, and they make events come alive.

All of the dialogue sounds lively, realistic, and appropriate.

There are no errors with quotation marks.

Using a Rubric to Study the Model

Discuss each question on the rubric with your classmates. Then use the rubric to assess Art Foley's historical fiction episode. Find sentences and paragraphs in it that help you answer each question.

How well does the writer hold the audience's interest throughout the story?

> I started to identify with Marco from the very first sentence, where I found out what his problem was. I was really wondering if his luck would change after he explained how he and his family were going to try to deal with the situation. Here is what he said to get me interested in how things would turn out.

"It's as hot here as it was in the desert," Marco said to himself. "But maybe our luck will change. Maybe we will be able to hire a boat that will get us at least as far as India."

How clearly does the story flow from beginning to middle to end?

" I think this story was easy to follow because it is just one specific episode, and the writer filled in the background necessary to understand the situation. We know the Polos have been having bad luck, so we read to find out if their luck has changed. The end of the story ties right into that question. "

I guess we haven't gotten rid of our bad luck yet, thought Marco. We will have to find another way to continue eastward.

How effectively does the writer use historical details to make the story sound authentic?

" I got a really good sense of what the Persian boats were like through the Polos' discussion with Omar. That whole part of the story is filled with historical details. Even their friend's name sounds very genuine! "

"Ask the captain how his ship can be seaworthy," Maffeo told Omar. "What happens if that single mast snaps in the wind? And what holds the boards together? I don't see any iron nails."

"Of course there aren't any nails," Omar responded. "Shipbuilders around here use wooden pegs, which work quite well. They stitch the planks together with strong threads made of coconut fibers. And the masts are lightweight and very flexible. . . ."

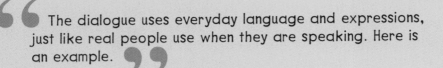
How realistic is the dialogue spoken by the characters?

The dialogue uses everyday language and expressions, just like real people use when they are speaking. Here is an example.

"Look at all the ships in this harbor," he insisted. "These captains and their crews cross back and forth to India every week. They will fall all over themselves trying to get your business."

How consistently does the writer use the correct punctuation for quotations?

There are no errors in the paper that I can see. And there are a lot of direct quotes, but they all seem to be punctuated and capitalized correctly. Take a look at these examples.

"Talk to that captain over there," Niccolò told Omar, "and ask if we can see his boat."

"An excellent choice," Omar praised him.

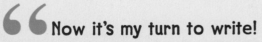 **Now it's my turn to write!**

I'm going to write my own historical fiction episode. Follow along as I work to see how I use good writing strategies. I'll be using the model and also the rubric to help me.

QuiANa

Writer of a Historical Fiction Episode

Name:	Quiana
Home:	Virginia
Hobbies:	going to museums, reading mystery stories (especially Edgar Allan Poe)
Favorite Athlete:	Arthur Ashe
Favorite Story:	"The Tell-Tale Heart" by Edgar Allan Poe
Assignment:	historical fiction episode

PreWriting

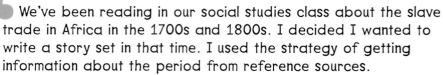

Gather

Use several references, including primary sources, to take notes about a historical period. Use the information to jot down story ideas.

" We've been reading in our social studies class about the slave trade in Africa in the 1700s and 1800s. I decided I wanted to write a story set in that time. I used the strategy of getting information about the period from reference sources.

"I started with an encyclopedia to get an overview. Then I went to the Internet, where I was lucky to find a great primary source: a slave's actual story of his capture and transport across the ocean. (You can't always find a primary source, so I felt lucky to have one.)

"As I did my research, I took notes on anything that I thought could be used in a story. Here are a few of my notes from my primary source, the narrative by captured slave Olaudah Equiano. "

Historical Period

A **historical period** is a time gone by. Colonial America, the 1960s, and the Victorian Age are all historical periods.

Primary Source

A **primary source** is a person or book that provides a firsthand account of the information. For example, a primary source about the Revolutionary War would be the journal, diary, or letter of a person who lived through the war. Here are two good ways to find primary sources:

- **Talk to an older person that you know.** Use this approach if you are writing about a recent historical period. The person may have firsthand experiences, or letters from older friends or relatives, to share with you.

- **Use the Internet.** Enter your topic idea in a good search engine, such as Yahoo or Google. The descriptions of the entries should help you see whether they include primary sources. Be sure you use only credible Web sites.

Slave trade in Africa—1700s and 1800s/Olaudah's capture

- families lived in fenced compounds, more than one building
- meals—goat stew, plantains, yams
- made clothes, rugs, etc on hand & foot loom
- when adults working in the fields, children often watching as lookouts from trees
- kidnapping pretty common
- Olaudah heard of prisoners shackled in dungeons
- kidnappers snuck over walls of their family compound, kidnapped Olaudah and his sister
- covered their mouths, carried them off into the woods

Story ideas

- Africa during slave trade—1760
- African family living in compound—family life
- brother and sister at home
- kidnappers in an African village

Go to page 18 in the **Practice** the Strategy **Notebook!**

Prewriting

Organize

Make a story map to organize my ideas.

" When I finished my research, I had an awful lot of information! Before I could use it in a story, I had to think of a simple plot I could develop without getting confused with all the details. I thought a good, exciting story might be about an African girl who manages to hide from some slave traders.

"My strategy was to organize my ideas with a story map. There's no set order for filling in a story map. I wrote in the plot/problem and the outcome first because I knew what they were. Then I looked through my notes for information about the setting and I filled that in. I found names for my major characters and also wrote down who the minor characters would be. I went back to my notes to get ideas for the major events of my episode. It actually turned out to be a little easier than I expected. "

Story Map

A **story map** organizes the setting, major and minor characters, plot and problem, major events, and outcome of the story.

Narrative Writing • Historical Fiction Episode

Setting:
Where: small village, not far from the coast in West Africa
When: 1760

Major Characters: Binta, a 12-year-old African girl
Diallo, her 10-year-old brother
Minor Characters: three slave traders
Binta and Diallo's mother

Plot/Problem:
A girl and her brother have to get away from some slave traders.

Event 1:
Binta and Diallo are left alone as their parents go to work in the fields.

Event 2:
Traders come into their village and toward their family compound.

Event 3:
The girl and her brother look for a place to hide.

Outcome:
The girl and her brother avoid being captured.

Go to page 20 in the **Practice the Strategy Notebook!**

Drafting

Write

Draft my story. Make sure it flows smoothly from beginning to middle to end.

"This is my thinking about getting my draft started. I know from the **Rubric** that a story should flow smoothly from start to finish. I know one way to do this is to tell events in the order they happened. But I wondered how else I could make all the parts fit together well.

"I looked at the model again to see what that writer did, and I noticed two things.

"First, he helped his audience by filling in a little background for the story. I knew my audience would mostly be students, so I decided I'd better do this, too.

"The other thing he did was to use the idea of bad luck to tie story parts together. I wondered if there was some big idea like this that I could use. I thought playing up one character's fear might work.

"I also decided to follow the model and use a third-person narrator, one who is not part of the story.

"In my first draft, I mainly concentrated just on telling my story. I'll take care of correcting mistakes later. Look on the next page to read my draft."

A Daring Escape

Binta was a twelve-year-old girl. She lived in a small village in West
Africa. She loved her parents and her brothers and sisters, and they
had many happy times together. But Binta was always afraid. ~~She was~~

There were many things that frightened Binta. She was afraid when
she had to light the fire to cook the family's food. She was afraid that
she could not do household chores well enough. Most of all, she was
afraid to be left alone when the older people ~~left~~ went out to work in
the fields. In that year, 1760, everybody knew that there were slave
traders around. They kidnaped healthy-looking young people and sold
them. A man from the villige had traveled down the river. He came back
and told everyone about a traders' fort.

One morning, Binta's mother was going out to work in the field as
usual. "Watch your little brother carefully, she said, and make sure he
stays inside our compound walls. Your father has heard that there are
traders around."

All at once Binta got very afraid, but she tried hard not to show it.
She promised that "she would take good care of her brother."

The morning went by, and nothing happened. Every half hour or so,
Binta had Diallo, her brother, climb the tall silk-cotton tree in their yard

to look for kidnappers, but except for the birds' screetches, the forest around the village was quiet. Binta was starting to relax in the afternoon when she sent Diallo up the tree one more time.

He had climbed about ten feet when he came scrambling back down. He had a terrifyed look on his face. "Sister, there are two men and a woman sneaking up to the village"! he whispered. "What shall we do?"

Binta was as frightened as her brother. For a minute she stood paralyzed. Then she could hear the kidnappers' careless talk.

"It is my impression that there are not any adults in the vicenity," one muttered to the others. "Let us attempt to locate some children."

"That is an excellent plan," said the woman's voice. "We shall examine what is behind that nearby wall. Be silent as we approach."

Binta and Diallo could hear the rustle of dry branches as the kidnappers came closer to the walls around their family compound.

"If they climb over, they're going to get us," said Diallo.

"But if we try to go out through the gate, they'll see us anyway," Binta replied. It seemed as if there was no escape.

Suddenly, Binta had an idea. "Remember that place behind Mother's quarters where we used to burrow under the fence? If we can get through there now, maybe we can hide in the forest until the kidnappers go away."

The small opening was on the opposite side of the compound from where the kidnappers were approaching. So Binta and Diallo had time to make their escape. Diallo went under first, then helped his sister squeeze through. Their compound was close enough to the forest that it was easy to get there and hide.

From their spot behind some low, thick bushes, Binta and Diallo could hear the kidnappers ransacking their family compound.

"I'm sure there were children here a minute ago," said the woman. "Where do you suppose they went?"

"Forget it," one of the men replied. "Let's try somewhere else."

Binta and Diallo stayed in the woods for a long time. Finally, when they heard their parents returning, they went back to the compound.

"Why were you outside?" Binta's mother said to her. "I told you to keep your brother safe from harm."

"That's just what I did, Mother," Binta replied. And as she thought about it, she knew she had reason to be proud. She had been afraid, but she did what she had to do anyway.

Go to page 21 in the Practice the Strategy Notebook!

Revising

Elaborate

Add historical details to make the story authentic.

READ TO A PARTNER

"When I finished my first draft, I read it to my partner, Brandon. Brandon liked a lot of my details describing the family compound. But he thought my story would be more interesting to my audience if I used more historical details at the beginning. My strategy was to go back to my notes, find a little more information, and add it to my paper."

Historical Detail

A **historical detail** is correct in its relationship to a certain time or place in history. For example, a historical detail would be a woman's use of a spinning wheel to make thread in colonial America. Historical details can make the story more realistic and meaningful for an audience.

[2nd DRAFT]

There were many things that frightened Binta. She was afraid
dinner of goat stew, plantains, and yams ← **historical detail**
when she had to light the fire to cook the family's food. She was
her cloth weaving on the hand-and-foot loom was not done ←
afraid that ~~she could not do household chores~~ well enough. Most of all,
she was afraid to be left alone when the older people went out to
work in the fields. In that year, 1760, everybody knew that there were
slave traders around. They kidnaped healthy-looking young people and
sold them. A man from the villige had traveled down the river. He came
back and told everyone about a traders' fort where prisoners were ←
shackled together and led, crying for mercy, into a dark underground
dungeon
historical detail

Go to page 23 in the Practice ∧the Strategy Notebook!

Narrative Writing • Historical Fiction Episode

Revising

Clarify — Make sure dialogue sounds realistic.

> I know from the **Rubric** that dialogue should sound realistic. Brandon thought that some of mine was pretty unnatural. So I made some changes there, too.

Dialogue

Dialogue is the talking that goes on between characters in a story. Here are some ways to make it sound natural.

- **Use contractions.** People usually say *I'm* and *you're* rather than *I am* and *you are*.

- **Use informal words and expressions.** People rarely use long, difficult words when they speak to each other.

  Formal: "I desire that you accompany me."

  Informal: "I want you to come with me."

- **Use idioms.** If not overused, idioms can liven up dialogue.

  "Please **keep an eye on** your brother," Mother said.

[3rd DRAFT]

"It ~~is my impression that~~ there ~~are not~~ any adults ~~in the vicenity~~," one muttered to the others. "~~Let us attempt to locate some children.~~" *looks like* / *aren't* / *around* / *Let's find us some children*

"~~That is an excellent plan~~," said the woman's voice. "~~We shall examine what is~~ behind that ~~nearby~~ wall. Be ~~silent as we approach~~." *Good idea* / *Let's see what's* / *over there* / *quiet now*

Go to page 24 in the **Practice the Strategy Notebook!**

Editing

Proofread

Check to see that quotations are punctuated correctly.

> It's time to look for errors in my story. I always check for misspelled words and poor grammar. But the **Rubric** also tells me to make sure I've punctuated quotations correctly. Sometimes I forget to capitalize them when I should, or to put quotation marks in the right places.

Direct Quotations

A **direct quotation** is the exact words of a speaker. A direct quotation begins and ends with quotation marks. If the quote is a sentence, it begins with a capital letter.

"**Those** men want to capture us," whispered Diallo.

When a comma, period, question mark, or exclamation mark ends a quote, that punctuation mark comes inside the quotation marks. A phrase identifying the speaker is set off with a comma.

"What should we do now**?**" the boy asked his sister.

Binta responded**,** "Stay quiet and they may not find us."

If a quotation is divided, both parts are enclosed in quotation marks. The second part is capitalized only if it is a new sentence.

"We'll find them," said the trader, "**if** it's the last thing we do."

"Didn't they go this way?" asked his partner. "**Let** me follow them."

An **indirect quotation**—someone reporting the speaker's words—is not set off with quotation marks.

Diallo asked his sister if she thought they would be safe.

Extra Practice
See **Direct Quotations** (pages CS 4-CS 5) in the back of this book.

Proofreading Marks

⌐ Indent.	ℓ Take out something.
≡ Make a capital.	⊙ Add a period.
/ Make a small letter.	# New paragraph
∧ Add something.	SP Spelling error

A Daring Escape

Binta was a twelve-year-old girl. She lived in a small village in West Africa. She loved her parents and her brothers and sisters, and they had many happy times together. But Binta was always afraid.

There were many things that frightened Binta. She was afraid when she had to light the fire to cook the family's dinner of goat stew, plantains, and yams. She was afraid that her cloth weaving on the hand-and-foot loom was not done well enough. Most of all, she was afraid to be left alone when the older people went out to work in the fields. In that year, 1760, everybody knew that there were slave traders around.

kidnapped SP

They kidnaped healthy-looking young people and sold them. A man from

village SP

the villige had traveled down the river. He came back and told everyone about a traders' fort where prisoners were shackled together and led, crying for mercy, into a dark underground dungeon.

quotation marks

quotation marks

One morning, Binta's mother was going out to work in the field as usual. "Watch your little brother carefully," she said, "and make sure he stays inside our compound walls. Your father has heard that there are traders around." ← quotation marks

indirect quotation

All at once Binta got very afraid, but she tried hard not to show it. She promised that "she would take good care of her brother."

The morning went by, and nothing happened. Every half hour or so, Binta had Diallo, her brother, climb the tall silk-cotton tree in their yard

SP screeches

to look for kidnappers, but except for the birds' screetches, the forest around the village was quiet. Binta was starting to relax in the afternoon when she sent Diallo up the tree one more time.

the Strategy

Go to page 25 in the **Practice Notebook!**

Publishing

Share

Include my story in a display that includes pictures and other articles about the time period.

Writer:	Quiana
Assignment:	historical fiction episode
Topic:	escaping the slave traders
Audience:	students and visitors to the school
Method of Publication:	hallway display case
Reason for Choice:	I learned so much about the period that I wanted to share what I knew with others.

“ Some students were preparing a display for Black History Month. They all liked my story and wanted to include it. Here's how I got it ready. ”

1. I reread my story one more time to make sure I had corrected all errors.

2. I drew pictures to illustrate my story.

3. I pasted each page onto a sheet of construction paper.

4. I tacked each page up in the display case separately so that other students could read my story easily.

A Daring Escape

by Quiana

Binta was a twelve-year-old girl. She lived in a small village in West Africa. She loved her parents and her brothers and sisters, and they had many happy times together. But Binta was always afraid.

There were many things that frightened Binta. She was afraid when she had to light the fire to cook the family's dinner of goat stew, plantains, and yams. She was afraid that her cloth weaving on the hand-and-foot loom was not done well enough. Most of all, she was afraid to be left alone when the older people went out to work in the fields. In that year, 1760, everybody knew that there were slave traders around. They kidnapped healthy-looking young people and sold them. A man from the village had traveled down the river. He came back and told everyone about a traders' fort where prisoners were shackled together and led, crying for mercy, into a dark underground dungeon.

One morning, Binta's mother was going out to work in the field as usual. "Watch your little brother carefully," she said, "and make sure he stays inside our compound walls. Your father has heard that there are traders around."

All at once Binta got very afraid, but she tried hard not to show it. She promised her mother that she would take good care of her brother.

The morning went by, and nothing happened. Every half hour or so, Binta had Diallo, her brother, climb the tall silk-cotton tree in their yard to look for kidnappers, but except for the birds' screeches, the forest around the village was quiet. Binta was starting to relax in the afternoon when she sent Diallo up the tree one more time.

He had climbed only about ten feet when he came scrambling back down. He had a terrified look on his face. "Sister, there are two men and a woman sneaking up to the village!" he whispered. "What shall we do?"

Binta was as frightened as her brother. For a minute she stood paralyzed. Then she could hear the kidnappers' careless talk.

"It looks like there aren't any adults around," one muttered to the others. "Let's find us some children."

"Good idea," said the woman's voice. "Let's see what's behind that wall over there. Be quiet now."

Binta and Diallo could hear the rustle of dry branches as the kidnappers came closer to the walls around their family compound.

"If they climb over, they're going to get us," said Diallo.

"But if we try to go out through the gate, they'll see us anyway," Binta replied. It seemed as if there was no escape.

Suddenly, Binta had an idea. "Remember that place behind Mother's quarters where we used to burrow under the fence? If we can get through there now, maybe we can hide in the forest until the kidnappers go away."

The small opening was on the opposite side of the compound from where the kidnappers were approaching. So Binta and Diallo had time to make their escape. Diallo went under first, then helped his sister squeeze through. Their compound was close enough to the forest that it was easy to get there and hide.

From their spot behind some low, thick bushes, Binta and Diallo could hear the kidnappers ransacking their family compound.

"I'm sure there were children here a minute ago," said the woman. "Where do you suppose they went?"

"Forget it," one of the men replied. "Let's try somewhere else."

Binta and Diallo stayed in the woods for a long time. Finally, when they heard their parents returning, they went back to the compound.

"Why were you outside?" Binta's mother said to her. "I told you to keep your brother safe from harm."

"That's just what I did, Mother," Binta replied. And as she thought about it, she knew she had reason to be proud. She had been afraid, but she did what she had to do anyway.

USING the Rubric for Assessment

Go to pages 26–27 in the Practice Notebook! Use that rubric to assess Quiana's paper. Try using the rubric to assess your own writing.

the Strategy

your own NARRATIVE writing

Responding to Literature

Put the strategies you practiced in this unit to work to write your own personal narrative, historical fiction episode, or both! You can:

- develop the Your Own Writing pages of the *Practice the Strategy Notebook*;
- pick an idea below and write something new;
- choose another idea of your own.

Be sure to follow the steps in the writing process. Use the rubrics in this unit to assess your writing.

Personal Narrative

- a time I got stage fright performing in a play
- a story or book I read that really made a difference in my life
- how I learned to like poetry

Historical Fiction Episode

- I went to the Alaskan Gold Rush with Sam McGee ("The Cremation of Sam McGee" by Robert William Service)
- living through the American Revolution (*Sarah Bishop* by Scott O'Dell)
- how the man who arrested a criminal named "Silky Bob" in New York got the job ("After Twenty Years" by O. Henry)

portfolio

School–Home Connection

Keep a writing portfolio. Think about adding the activities from the *Practice the Strategy Notebook* to your writing portfolio. You may want to take your portfolio home to share.

EXPOSITORY writing

shares knowledge by presenting and explaining information.

1

E-Mail

2

Summary

E-Mail

This chapter will focus on one kind of expository writing, an **e-mail**.

An **e-mail** (or electronic mail) is a written message that a writer sends to a reader through a computer network.

The piece of writing on the next page is an e-mail. Read these questions. Then read the message. Keep the questions in mind as you read.

 How clearly and politely does the writer communicate with the audience (the reader of the e-mail)?

 How effectively has the writer used order of importance in organizing questions or comments?

 How well has the writer explained the purpose of the e-mail in the introduction and the importance of getting an answer to it in the conclusion?

 How well does the writer observe good e-mail etiquette?

 How accurately does the writer use past and past participle forms of verbs?

Address http://www.mayohealth.org/home?id=2.1.1

Subject Questions about antibiotics

Date: Wed, 5 April 2000
From: mkubik@surprise.net

I have a few questions about antibiotics. I hope you can answer them. Just last week my doctor gave me an antibiotic prescription for an ear infection. I need information about that. Also, I have heard some interesting (and frightening) things about antibiotics lately. Here are my questions:

1. Why does a person need to take 10 or 14 pills when an infection often seems to go away after 3 or 4 pills? For example, it feels like my ear infection is gone now. But my doctor told me to take all the pills.

2. I've heard that antibiotics work only on bacteria-based infections. They do not work on viruses, such as colds. Could you explain why this is true?

3. I read that some pretty awful bacteria-based illnesses are resistant to antibiotics. The list included pneumonia and tuberculosis. How can this be? I thought antibiotics cured all bacterial infections.

Please respond at your earliest possible convenience. I really am not sure if I need to continue with my prescription. Your advice would be greatly appreciated. I would also appreciate answers to my other questions.

Mary Kubik
mkubik@surprise.net

Using a Rubric

A rubric is a tool that lists "what counts" for a piece of writing.

How does a rubric work? You assign 1, 2, 3, or 4 points to qualities in a piece of writing to show how well the author dealt with them. The questions on page 60 were used to make this rubric.

"Hi! My name is Charlotte. I'm learning about writing e-mails, too. What did you think of the e-mail you just read? Read this rubric. Start with the questions. Then read the information for each question. We'll use the rubric to evaluate the e-mail."

Audience

How clearly and politely does the writer communicate with the audience (the reader of the e-mail)?

Organization

How effectively has the writer used order of importance in organizing questions or comments?

Elaboration

How well has the writer explained the purpose of the e-mail in the introduction and the importance of getting an answer to it in the conclusion?

Clarification

How well does the writer observe good e-mail etiquette?

Conventions & Skills

How accurately does the writer use past and past participle forms of verbs?

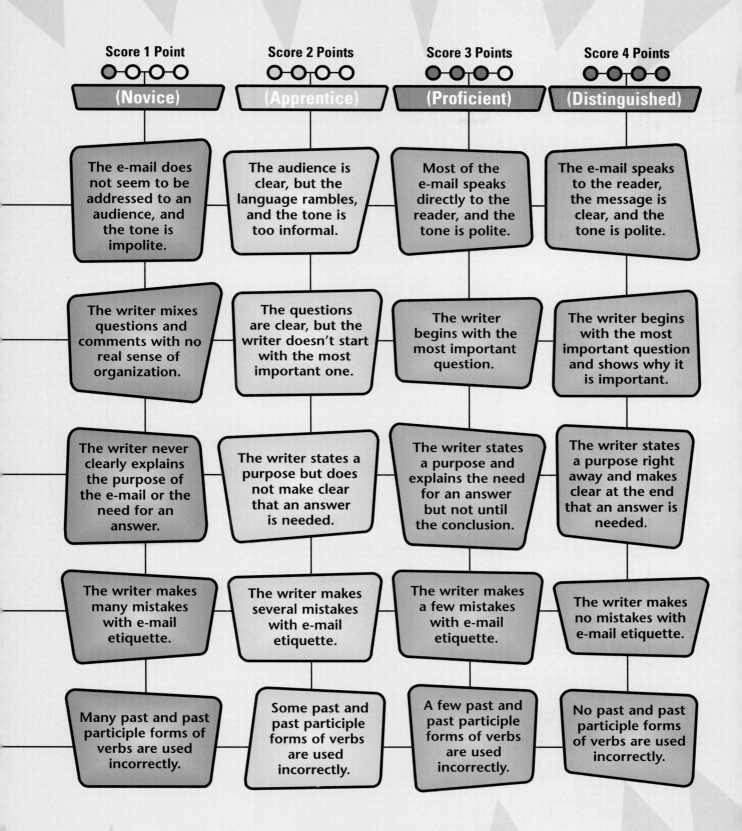

Score 1 Point
(Novice)

Score 2 Points
(Apprentice)

Score 3 Points
(Proficient)

Score 4 Points
(Distinguished)

The e-mail does not seem to be addressed to an audience, and the tone is impolite.

The audience is clear, but the language rambles, and the tone is too informal.

Most of the e-mail speaks directly to the reader, and the tone is polite.

The e-mail speaks to the reader, the message is clear, and the tone is polite.

The writer mixes questions and comments with no real sense of organization.

The questions are clear, but the writer doesn't start with the most important one.

The writer begins with the most important question.

The writer begins with the most important question and shows why it is important.

The writer never clearly explains the purpose of the e-mail or the need for an answer.

The writer states a purpose but does not make clear that an answer is needed.

The writer states a purpose and explains the need for an answer but not until the conclusion.

The writer states a purpose right away and makes clear at the end that an answer is needed.

The writer makes many mistakes with e-mail etiquette.

The writer makes several mistakes with e-mail etiquette.

The writer makes a few mistakes with e-mail etiquette.

The writer makes no mistakes with e-mail etiquette.

Many past and past participle forms of verbs are used incorrectly.

Some past and past participle forms of verbs are used incorrectly.

A few past and past participle forms of verbs are used incorrectly.

No past and past participle forms of verbs are used incorrectly.

Using a Rubric to Study the Model

With your classmates, discuss each question on the rubric. Find sentences and paragraphs in the model that help you answer each question. Then use the rubric to assess Mary Kubik's e-mail.

Audience

How clearly and politely does the writer communicate with the audience (the reader of the e-mail)?

" The writer knows that a question column in a Web site may get thousands of e-mails, so she makes her message very specific and to the point. She speaks directly to her reader and is very polite. "

Please respond at your earliest possible convenience. . . . Your advice would be greatly appreciated.

Organization How effectively has the writer used order of importance in organizing questions or comments?

" The most important question to this writer is the one about whether she should keep on taking the antibiotic, so she puts that question first. "

1. Why does a person need to take 10 or 14 pills when an infection often seems to go away after 3 or 4 pills? For example, it feels like my ear infection is gone now. But my doctor told me to take all the pills.

Elaboration How well has the writer explained the purpose of the e-mail in the introduction and the importance of getting an answer to it in the conclusion?

" The writer explains her purpose right away, in the opening paragraph. Then, after she's asked her questions, she tells why she needs a quick answer to at least one of them. "

I really am not sure if I need to continue with my prescription. Your advice would be greatly appreciated. I would also appreciate answers to my other questions.

How well does the writer observe good e-mail etiquette?

" I know that most e-mail is more like conversation than snail mail, but it still needs to be polite. The writer seems to follow e-mail etiquette very well. She doesn't put words in capital letters to look like shouting or use any fancy type. Her subject line is clear, and she remembers to put her name at the end of the e-mail. Have a look. "

Subject: Questions about antibiotics
Mary Kubik
mkubik@surprise.net

How accurately does the writer use past and past participle forms of verbs?

" The writer uses verb forms correctly, even those with past and past participle forms that sometimes confuse me. Here are a few examples.

Just last week my doctor gave me an antibiotic prescription for an ear infection. . . . Also, I have heard some interesting . . . things about antibiotics lately.

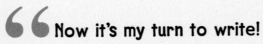

" **Now it's my turn to write!**

I'm going to write my own e-mail. Follow along to see how I use the model and also the rubric to help me with good writing strategies. "

Charlotte

Writer of an E-Mail

Name: Charlotte
Home: Georgia
Hobbies and Interests: reading, Jojo (pet cat)
Favorite Book: *Anne of Green Gables* by Lucy Maud Montgomery
Favorite Food: any kind of fish and starting to like peaches
Assignment: e-mail

Prewriting

Gather
Use an Internet search engine to find credible Web sites that can answer questions about my hobby or interest.

"Ever since I moved here from Maine, I've noticed that people, especially older people, use words and expressions that are different from what I'm used to. As a result, I've gotten very interested in dialect. (That's the way language is spoken in a particular region.) I decided to contact a Web site that would answer some of my dialect questions.

"I started with a search engine. The one I used came up with more than 100 Web sites on my topic! My strategy was to choose only credible ones, and I was lucky. One of the first sites I found was run by the American Dialect Society. It included an e-mail address where you could send questions."

Search Engine

A **search engine** is a program that searches for things on the Web. Enter a topic name or key words into a search engine, and it gives you a list of Web sites that include those words.

Credible Web Site

A **credible Web site** is a place on the Internet that can generally be trusted to have correct information. An example is *www.britannica.com*, a Web site run by Encyclopedia Britannica. Here are some other credible sites:

- sites run by universities or other educational institutions (they end in *.edu*)
- sites run by U.S. government agencies or national organizations (they end in *.gov* or *.org*)
- sites run by print newspapers (for example, the *New York Times*), by PBS, or by the news departments of television networks

Go to page 28 in the **Practice the Strategy Notebook!**

Prewriting

Organize
List, in order of importance, three questions to ask the Web site about my topic.

"I had a lot of things I wanted to know about dialect, but I realized my e-mail couldn't be too long. So I put what I wanted to know into three general questions. I knew from the **Rubric** to organize them by order of importance, so I tried to figure out which question was the most important to me. I used the order-of-importance organizer to help me line up my ideas."

Order-of-Importance Organizer

An **order-of-importance organizer** shows the features of a topic in order of importance. It begins with the most important feature and moves to the least important feature.

Order-of-Importance Organizer

Most important
why people speak differently in different parts of the country

Next in importance
words and expressions I've never heard before (**fixing to, tote,** etc.)

Least important
why TV announcers sound so perfect

Go to page 30 in the **Practice the Strategy Notebook!**

Drafting

Draft the body of my e-mail. Put my questions into a clear format.

" To draft my e-mail, I looked at the model. I noticed that the whole middle section, or body, of Mary Kubik's e-mail was made up of her questions. To make them stand out, she numbered each one. Because one of my questions had three parts, I decided to use numbers there instead. The strategy I was following was to use a clear and to-the-point format, and this seemed like the best way to do it.

"I drafted my e-mail right on the computer. I spent a fair amount of time formatting my questions. I did the best I could with grammar and spelling, but I didn't worry too much about them at this point. I knew I could fix these kinds of errors later. "

Address http://www.americandialect.org/submit.shtml

Subject Questions about dialect

Date: Mon, 14 May 20--

From: chlewis@surprise.net

[1st DRAFT]

Hi! How are all you dialect folks doin'? I'm a seventh-grade girl who recently moved to the South from Maine. I need help!

First of all, how does dialect happen? When I say things to people like "I'm in a terrible wacket," they have no idea what I mean. And there are things they say that I've never heard before. What's going on, dude? Until I moved here, I thought that English was the same everywhere.

I've wrote some words and espressions below that I'd like to know more about:

1. People here say "I'm fixing to" a lot. Can you tell me what it means? I can't find it in my dicshunary.

2. It seems as if evening starts right after lunch here. Is that something that was brung here from England? I've never heard of that way of speaking before.

3. I've noticed that people tote things instead of carrying them. Is that why we have tote bags? Do people say "tote" in a lot of other places?

One more question: since I begun paying attention to language, I've noticed that anouncers on TV don't talk like Southerners OR people from my part of New england. Why does their speech sound so PERFECT?

I'm beginning to think that English is VERY complicated. :- (

Charlotte

Go to page 31 in the **Practice** the Strategy **Notebook!**

Revising

Elaborate

Check that my tone is appropriate and that my introduction and conclusion fulfill their purpose.

> When I read through my e-mail, I used the strategy of checking for appropriate tone, introduction, and conclusion. Right away I noticed that the beginning of my paper needed help! My introduction didn't make my reason for writing clear at all. And some of my sentences didn't have the right tone for a serious note to someone I didn't even know. In my conclusion, I had forgotten to ask for answers to my questions. So I went back and made some changes.

Tone

Tone is the writer's attitude toward the subject of his or her writing. A writer's tone can be serious, funny, sarcastic, objective, and so on.

Introduction, Conclusion

The **introduction** is the first paragraph of a paper. A good introduction grabs the audience's attention and states the main idea of the paper.

In an e-mail, the introduction gets to the point very quickly. It is concise and direct and does not waste the reader's time.

The **conclusion** is the last paragraph of a longer paper. The conclusion may tie up loose ends and summarize main points.

In an e-mail requesting information, the conclusion tells the reader what is wanted and politely requests a response.

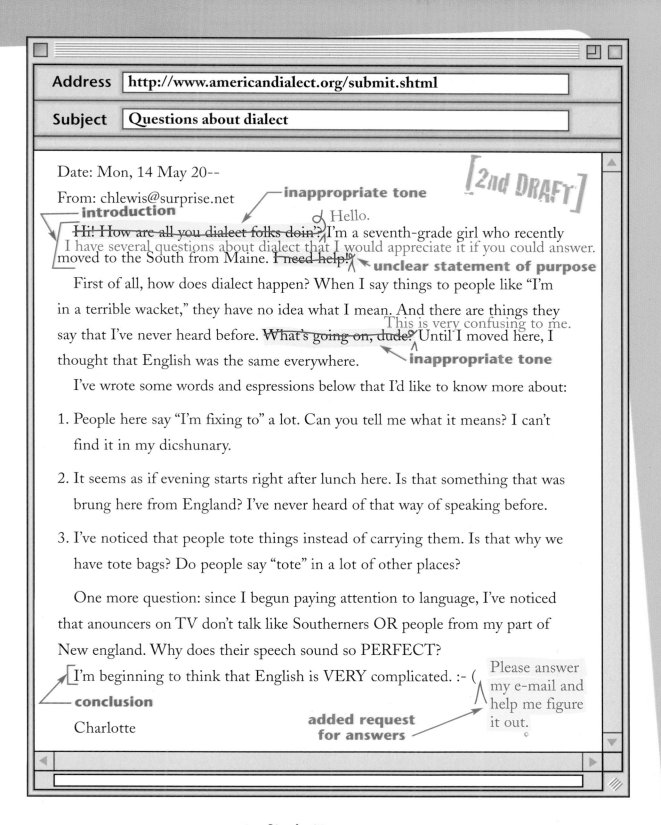

Address http://www.americandialect.org/submit.shtml

Subject Questions about dialect

[2nd DRAFT]

Date: Mon, 14 May 20--

From: chlewis@surprise.net

— *inappropriate tone*

— *introduction*

~~Hi! How are all you dialect folks doin'?~~ Hello. I'm a seventh-grade girl who recently moved to the South from Maine. ~~I need help!~~ I have several questions about dialect that I would appreciate it if you could answer.

← *unclear statement of purpose*

First of all, how does dialect happen? When I say things to people like "I'm in a terrible wacket," they have no idea what I mean. And there are things they say that I've never heard before. ~~What's going on, dude?~~ This is very confusing to me. Until I moved here, I thought that English was the same everywhere.

— *inappropriate tone*

I've wrote some words and espressions below that I'd like to know more about:

1. People here say "I'm fixing to" a lot. Can you tell me what it means? I can't find it in my dicshunary.

2. It seems as if evening starts right after lunch here. Is that something that was brung here from England? I've never heard of that way of speaking before.

3. I've noticed that people tote things instead of carrying them. Is that why we have tote bags? Do people say "tote" in a lot of other places?

One more question: since I begun paying attention to language, I've noticed that anouncers on TV don't talk like Southerners OR people from my part of New england. Why does their speech sound so PERFECT?

I'm beginning to think that English is VERY complicated. :- (Please answer my e-mail and help me figure it out.

— *conclusion*

Charlotte

added request for answers →

Go to page 33 in the **Practice** the Strategy **Notebook!**

Revising

Clarify
Make sure that I have observed good e-mail etiquette.

"The **Rubric** makes it clear that good e-mail etiquette is important. I checked mine and found a few things that needed correcting. For example, I did a little "shouting" toward the end of the e-mail, and I forgot to give my full name at the end."

E-Mail Etiquette

E-mail etiquette is the most polite, most accepted, or clearest way to write an e-mail message. To follow good e-mail etiquette, do the following:

- Write a subject line that clearly identifies what the e-mail is about.

- Do not use any charts or special type features (for example, bullets, italic type, or underlining) in your e-mail, because most e-mail programs will not be able to translate them.

- Do not use emoticons (such as :-) for a happy face or :-(for a sad face) unless you are writing to someone you know well.

- Do not use all capital letters, except when absolutely necessary. They are hard to read and make the writer appear to be "shouting."

- Include a salutation when you know to whom you are writing. Put your full name and e-mail address at the end of formal e-mails, since e-mail addresses often do not clearly identify the sender.

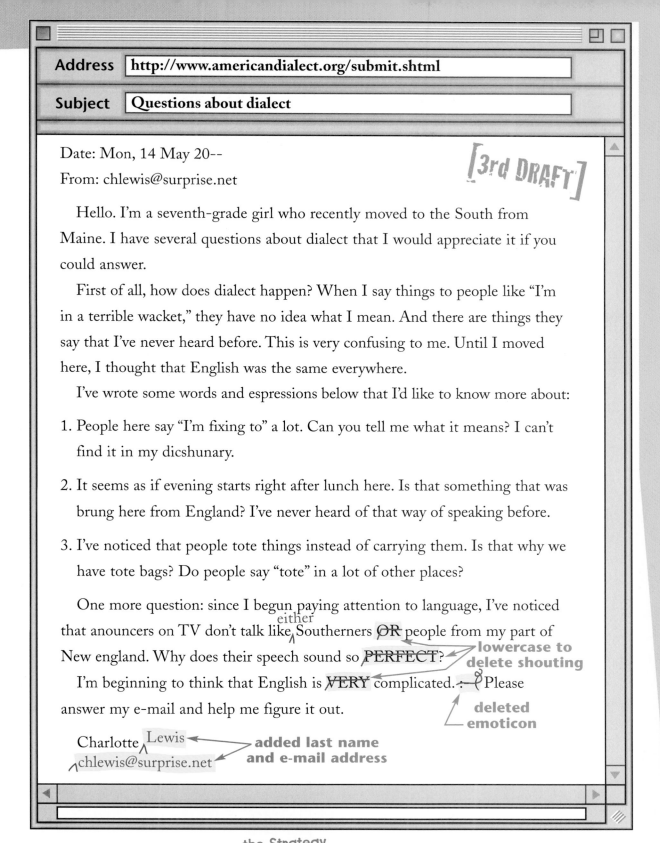

Address http://www.americandialect.org/submit.shtml

Subject Questions about dialect

[3rd DRAFT]

Date: Mon, 14 May 20--

From: chlewis@surprise.net

Hello. I'm a seventh-grade girl who recently moved to the South from Maine. I have several questions about dialect that I would appreciate it if you could answer.

First of all, how does dialect happen? When I say things to people like "I'm in a terrible wacket," they have no idea what I mean. And there are things they say that I've never heard before. This is very confusing to me. Until I moved here, I thought that English was the same everywhere.

I've wrote some words and espressions below that I'd like to know more about:

1. People here say "I'm fixing to" a lot. Can you tell me what it means? I can't find it in my dicshunary.

2. It seems as if evening starts right after lunch here. Is that something that was brung here from England? I've never heard of that way of speaking before.

3. I've noticed that people tote things instead of carrying them. Is that why we have tote bags? Do people say "tote" in a lot of other places?

One more question: since I begun paying attention to language, I've noticed that anouncers on TV don't talk like either Southerners OR people from my part of New england. Why does their speech sound so PERFECT?   lowercase to delete shouting

I'm beginning to think that English is VERY complicated. :-(Please   deleted emoticon
answer my e-mail and help me figure it out.

Charlotte Lewis   ← added last name
chlewis@surprise.net   and e-mail address

Go to page 34 in the **Practice** the Strategy **Notebook!**

Editing

Proofread

Check the e-mail address. Be sure that past and past participle verb forms are used correctly.

" Now I need to look for errors. First I double-check the e-mail address. The **Rubric** also reminds me to make sure I've used past and past participle verb forms correctly. There are a few verbs that sometimes give me trouble. "

Conventions & SKILLS

Past and Past Participle Verb Forms

The **past** form of a verb is the form that is used alone to tell about something in the past. The **past participle** form is used with a helping verb such as *have, has, had, is,* or *was.*

Past Form: I **gave** my teacher the note from the dialect Web site.

Past Participle Form: She **has given** me a lot of support for my dialect project.

Many verbs, called **irregular verbs,** have different forms in the past and past participle. Here are some of the most common ones:

Present	Past	Past Participle
go	went	(has, have) gone
begin	began	(has, have) begun
bring	brought	(has, have) brought
see	saw	(has, have) seen
eat	ate	(has, have) eaten
speak	spoke	(has, have) spoken
come	came	(has, have) come
write	wrote	(has, have) written
choose	chose	(has, have) chosen
run	ran	(has, have) run
wear	wore	(has, have) worn
do	did	(has, have) done

If you are not sure of the correct forms of a verb, check a dictionary.

Extra Practice
See **Past and Past Participle Verb Forms** (pages CS 6–CS 7) in the back of this book.

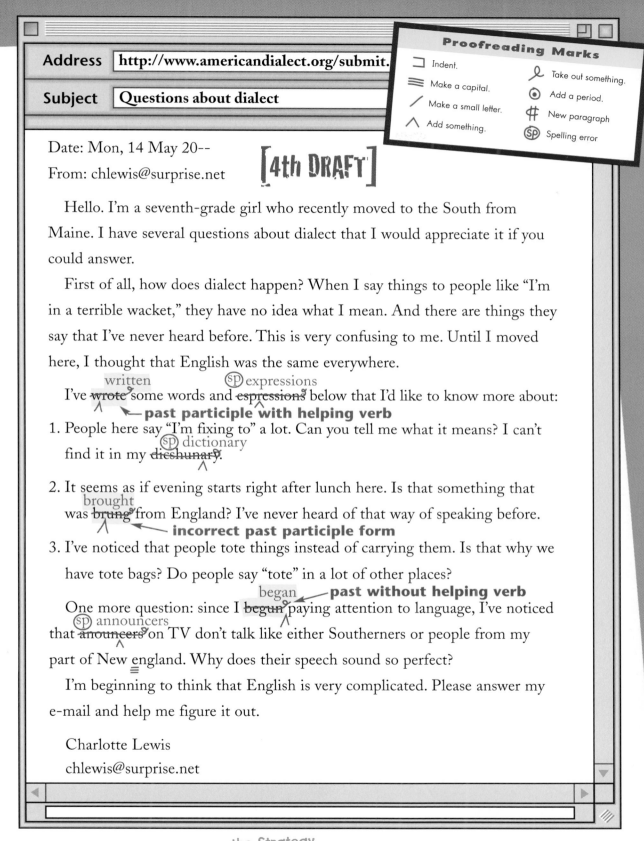

Proofreading Marks

⌐ Indent.

☰ Make a capital.

/ Make a small letter.

∧ Add something.

ℒ Take out something.

⊙ Add a period.

New paragraph

ⓢⓟ Spelling error

Address http://www.americandialect.org/submit.

Subject **Questions about dialect**

Date: Mon, 14 May 20--

From: chlewis@surprise.net **[4th DRAFT]**

Hello. I'm a seventh-grade girl who recently moved to the South from Maine. I have several questions about dialect that I would appreciate it if you could answer.

First of all, how does dialect happen? When I say things to people like "I'm in a terrible wacket," they have no idea what I mean. And there are things they say that I've never heard before. This is very confusing to me. Until I moved here, I thought that English was the same everywhere.

I've ~~wrote~~ written some words and ~~espressions~~ ⓢⓟ expressions below that I'd like to know more about: ← **past participle with helping verb**

1. People here say "I'm fixing to" a lot. Can you tell me what it means? I can't find it in my ~~dieshunary~~ ⓢⓟ dictionary.

2. It seems as if evening starts right after lunch here. Is that something that was ~~brung~~ brought from England? I've never heard of that way of speaking before. ← **incorrect past participle form**

3. I've noticed that people tote things instead of carrying them. Is that why we have tote bags? Do people say "tote" in a lot of other places?

One more question: since I ~~begun~~ began paying attention to language, I've noticed — **past without helping verb** that ~~anouncers~~ ⓢⓟ announcers on TV don't talk like either Southerners or people from my part of New england. Why does their speech sound so perfect?

I'm beginning to think that English is very complicated. Please answer my e-mail and help me figure it out.

Charlotte Lewis

chlewis@surprise.net

Go to page 35 in the **Practice** the Strategy **Notebook!**

Publishing

Share   Send my e-mail to the Web site.

Writer:	Charlotte
Assignment:	e-mail
Topic:	questions about dialect
Audience:	person who answers questions at Web site
Method of Publication:	send via the Internet
Reason for Choice:	I found a Web site that I thought could accurately answer my questions.

> **"** I knew I had picked a good site to send my questions to, so I just had to get my e-mail into final form. Here's what I did to get it ready. **"**

1. I typed up my e-mail on my e-mail server.

2. I read through my message again to be sure it was as good as I could make it.

3. After checking the site's e-mail address one more time, I pushed "send."

4. I waited to make sure the message actually went through and was not returned to me.

5. I checked every day for a response. (Yesterday I got one!)

Address http://www.americandialect.org/submit.shtml

Subject Questions about dialect

Date: Mon, 14 May 20--
From: chlewis@surprise.net

Hello. I'm a seventh-grade girl who recently moved to the South from Maine. I have several questions about dialect that I would appreciate it if you could answer.

First of all, how does dialect happen? When I say things to people like "I'm in a terrible wacket," they have no idea what I mean. And there are things they say that I've never heard before. This is very confusing to me. Until I moved here, I thought that English was the same everywhere.

I've written some words and expressions below that I'd like to know more about:

1. People here say "I'm fixing to" a lot. Can you tell me what it means? I can't find it in my dictionary.

2. It seems as if evening starts right after lunch here. Is that something that was brought from England? I've never heard of that way of speaking before.

3. I've noticed that people tote things instead of carrying them. Is that why we have tote bags? Do people say "tote" in a lot of other places?

One more question: since I began paying attention to language, I've noticed that announcers on TV don't talk like either Southerners or people from my part of New England. Why does their speech sound so perfect?

I'm beginning to think that English is very complicated. Please answer my e-mail and help me figure it out.

Charlotte Lewis
chlewis@surprise.net

USING the Rubric for Assessment

Go to pages 36–37 in the **Practice Notebook!** Use that ∧ the Strategy rubric to assess Charlotte's e-mail. Try using the rubric to assess your own writing.

EXPOSITORY writing

Summary

In this chapter, you will have a chance to do one kind of expository writing, a **summary**.

A **summary** is a short piece of writing that pulls out the main points from a longer selection and combines them to tell what the selection is about. A summary is always considerably shorter than the selection it summarizes, and it is written in your own words.

On the next three pages, you will find a summary and the magazine article on which it is based. First, read the questions below. Then read the summary and the article, keeping the questions in mind as you read.

 **Audience** How well does the summary convey the important points of the article to the audience?

 **Organization** How concisely does the writer organize and explain the article's main ideas?

 **Elaboration** Does the summary stay focused on main points and avoid information that is too detailed?

 **Clarification** Has the writer used verbs in the active voice appropriately?

 **Conventions & Skills** How consistently does the writer provide clear antecedents and use correct pronoun forms?

"The Structure That Never Sleeps"
by Kim Williams

Summary by Lidia Peretsky

The Romans did not invent the arch. However, they were the first people who really knew how to build it, and they influenced people who came after them. Before the Romans, people built square rather than curved openings.

The Romans often built freestanding arches to celebrate great victories. Such arches were huge and visible from great distances. "Triumphal" arches of this type have been built in many places around the world.

Today you will find arches in all kinds of modern buildings and structures. They can be built with a variety of materials and in a variety of shapes and sizes. Besides being useful to us, arches also capture our imaginations.

The Structure That Never Sleeps
by Kim Williams

As tributes to especially important victories or as tributes to the greatness of the emperors themselves, special monumental arches called triumphal arches were erected in Rome. The Arch of Titus was built in A.D. 81 to celebrate Emperor Titus's capture of Jerusalem in A.D. 70, and the Arch of Constantine was built in A.D. 312 and 315 to celebrate Emperor Constantine's victory over his rival and brother-in-law, Emperor Maxentius. These were free-standing arches. That is, they stood alone without being part of a wall and were placed in prominent positions so that they could be seen from very far away.

Why did the Romans choose the arch as a symbol of triumph? It may be because the arch represented the triumph of Roman engineering over the most difficult structural problems.

The architects of ancient Egypt and Greece knew about the arch, but their architecture was mostly trabeated, based on vertical columns spanned by horizontal, flat beams. The Romans didn't invent the arch; they adopted the form from the architecture of the Etruscans, the people who ruled Italy before the beginning of the Roman Republic in the sixth century B.C. But to their credit, the Romans perfected the techniques of arch construction, making Roman architecture different from anything that came before it. It was because they understood the techniques of arch construction that Roman architects would later be able to develop even more complicated structures, such as the vault and the dome.

Even though the Roman Empire eventually collapsed in the fifth century A.D., its architecture continued to have a huge influence in later centuries. Triumphal arches were built long after there were no more Roman emperors. Perhaps the most famous triumphal arch of all is the Arc de Triomphe in Paris, commissioned by Napoleon Bonaparte in 1806 to honor the Grand Army and completed in 1836.

In the United States, the Washington Arch was built in New York City's Washington Square to celebrate the one-hundred-year anniversary of the inauguration of George Washington as President of the United States. Actually, there were two Washington arches. The first one, built in 1889, was a temporary arch made of wood and plaster, and was intended to be taken down when the celebration ended. New Yorkers, however, liked the arch so much that it was soon decided to build a permanent one in marble. This one was dedicated in 1895.

Today, arches are found everywhere. Small arches can be used as doors, and large ones as bridges. Arches can be built of brick, stone, concrete, or steel. They don't have to be round, either, but can be made in lots of special shapes. In addition to their usefulness, arches still have the power to capture our imaginations.

One such arch stands on the banks of the Mississippi River in St. Louis, Missouri. The "Gateway to the West" was designed in the late 1940s by architect Eero Saarinen to honor Thomas Jefferson and the expansion of the United States to the west. Topped off in 1965 and dedicated in 1968, the Gateway Arch has the form of a catenary curve. (If you hold each end of a chain and let it droop between your hands, you have created a catenary curve.) As high as a sixty-three-story building, the carbon-steel arch is covered in gleaming stainless steel. A special kind of tram carries visitors to the top.

Of all the ways that architects have invented of going from "here" to "there," the sweeping curves of the arch may be the most beautiful. Now that you know about arches, look around you. You're sure to find these lovely shapes in your town or city, too.

Using a Rubric

A rubric is a tool that tells "what counts" in a piece of writing.

How do you use a rubric? You assign 1, 2, 3, or 4 points to qualities in the writing. These points show how well the author dealt with the various qualities.

The questions on page 80 were used to make this rubric.

"Hi! My name is Paul. I'm learning about summaries, too. What did you think of the summary on page 81? Take a look at this rubric. Begin with the questions; then go on to read the information for each question. We'll be using the rubric to evaluate the summary you just read."

Audience

How well does the summary convey the important points of the article to the audience?

Organization

How concisely does the writer organize and explain the article's main ideas?

Elaboration

Does the summary stay focused on main points and avoid information that is too detailed?

Clarification

Has the writer used verbs in the active voice appropriately?

Conventions & Skills

How consistently does the writer provide clear antecedents and use correct pronoun forms?

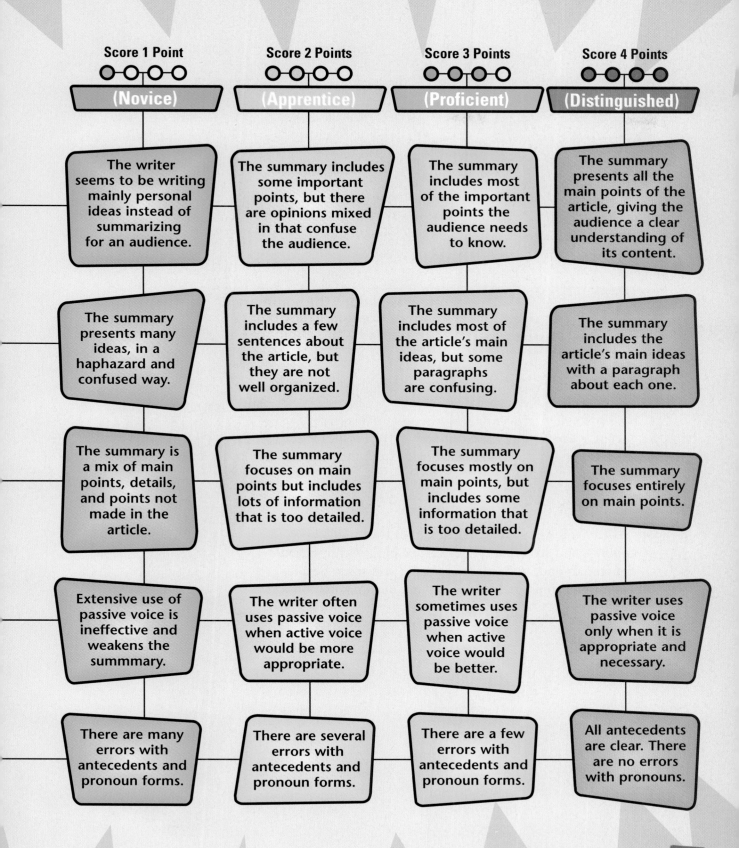

Score 1 Point

(Novice)

The writer seems to be writing mainly personal ideas instead of summarizing for an audience.

The summary presents many ideas, in a haphazard and confused way.

The summary is a mix of main points, details, and points not made in the article.

Extensive use of passive voice is ineffective and weakens the summmary.

There are many errors with antecedents and pronoun forms.

Score 2 Points

(Apprentice)

The summary includes some important points, but there are opinions mixed in that confuse the audience.

The summary includes a few sentences about the article, but they are not well organized.

The summary focuses on main points but includes lots of information that is too detailed.

The writer often uses passive voice when active voice would be more appropriate.

There are several errors with antecedents and pronoun forms.

Score 3 Points

(Proficient)

The summary includes most of the important points the audience needs to know.

The summary includes most of the article's main ideas, but some paragraphs are confusing.

The summary focuses mostly on main points, but includes some information that is too detailed.

The writer sometimes uses passive voice when active voice would be better.

There are a few errors with antecedents and pronoun forms.

Score 4 Points

(Distinguished)

The summary presents all the main points of the article, giving the audience a clear understanding of its content.

The summary includes the article's main ideas with a paragraph about each one.

The summary focuses entirely on main points.

The writer uses passive voice only when it is appropriate and necessary.

All antecedents are clear. There are no errors with pronouns.

Using a **Rubric** to Study the Model

Discuss each question on the rubric with your classmates. Then use the rubric to assess Lidia Peretsky's summary. Find sentences and paragraphs in it that help you answer each question.

 **Audience**

How well does the summary convey the important points of the article to the audience?

" I think the audience will understand the article. The writer did a good job of presenting information accurately and clearly. For example, her explanation of modern arches is simple, but it gives the basic facts that the reader needs to know. "

Today you will find arches in all kinds of modern buildings and structures. They can be built with a variety of materials and in a variety of shapes and sizes. Besides being useful to us, arches also capture our imaginations.

How concisely does the writer organize and explain the article's main ideas?

"The writer wrote three short paragraphs about the same three main ideas that I noticed in the article. Each paragraph gives important supporting details about its main idea. Here is what the writer covers in each paragraph."

Paragraph 1: history of the arch
Paragraph 2: triumphal arches
Paragraph 3: the variety of modern arches

Does the summary stay focused on main points and avoid information that is too detailed?

"The article includes several specific examples of arches, but these are details that don't need to be in a summary. So the writer only mentions these arches in a general way."

"Triumphal" arches of this type have been built in many places around the world.

Clarification

Has the writer used verbs in the active voice appropriately?

"I noticed that there were a few places where the writer couldn't use active voice. For instance, once she had to say 'have been built' because she didn't know who did the building. As often as possible, though, she used active voice. Look at these sentences."

Before the Romans, people built square rather than curved openings.

Today you will find arches in all kinds of modern buildings and structures.

Conventions & Skills

How consistently does the writer provide clear antecedents and use correct pronoun forms?

"I didn't see any errors at all with pronoun forms in this summary. I also noticed that I could easily pick out the antecedents for pronouns. In this example it's easy to tell that **they** refers to the Romans."

The Romans did not invent the arch. However, they were the first people who really knew how to build it. . . .

" Now it's my turn to write!

I'm going to write my own summary. Watch me as I work to see how I use the model and also the rubric to help me practice good writing strategies. "

PauL

Writer of a Summary

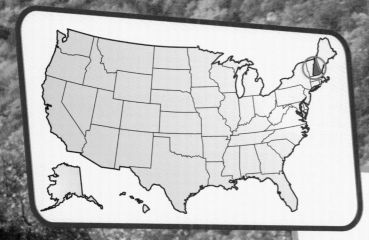

Name: Paul

Home: New Hampshire

Hobbies: hiking in the mountains, cooking with my father

Favorite Food: anything hot!

Favorite Book: *Salsas, Sambals, Chutneys, and Chowchows* by Chris Schlesinger and John Willoughby

Assignment: summary

PreWriting

Gather

Read an article on a topic that interests me. Jot down the 5 W's from the article.

> When my teacher told us we could write a summary of any informational article from a magazine, I got pretty excited. I had just read a really interesting article about spicy food, and I knew I could write a good summary of it. Here is the article I read.

What's So Hot About Spices?

by Gail Jarrow and Paul Sherman

Sour pork curry from India. Spicy shrimp from Vietnam. Hot tamales from Mexico. Spicy foods seem to come from countries with a tropical climate.

Two scientists, Jennifer Billing and Dr. Paul Sherman, wondered why. They thought that healthy eating habits probably helped people survive. But how could eating spicy foods in hot climates make diners healthier?

Spices come from plant parts: leaves, flowers, fruits, seeds, or roots. (Salt isn't a true spice since it doesn't come from a plant.) Chemicals in spice plants have aromas and tastes that people like.

The desire for spices was so great that it affected the course of history. The Arabs, Phoenicians, and Europeans explored the world in search of shortcuts to tropical regions of Asia, where many of the popular spices grew. Christopher Columbus was looking for such a shortcut when he bumped into America.

Without refrigeration, foods spoil quickly and can cause illness. Since ancient times, people have used spices to keep food from spoiling—to preserve it. The Romans used red cumin and coriander. Pirates preserved wild game for sea travel by smoking it and rubbing it with allspice. The Egyptians also knew that spices could prevent decay. They even used them in mummification.

Strong Chemicals

Hundreds of years ago people didn't know how certain spices preserved foods. Since then, scientists have discovered that spices contain powerful chemicals. These chemicals protect the spice plants from bacteria, insects, fungi, and hungry animals. When we use spices, the same chemicals prevent the growth of bacteria that spoil our food and can sometimes make us sick.

Scientists have tested thirty spices on dozens of food-spoiling bacteria. Every spice affected at least one type of bacterium. The super bacteria killers were allspice, garlic, onion, and oregano. These spices killed or slowed the growth of all bacteria on which they were tested.

Some spices aren't so appealing—at least until you get used to them. You probably wouldn't cover yourself with the scent of garlic or onion if you were trying to impress your friends. Eating fresh hot peppers and chilies can blister your mouth.

Then why did people start eating foods seasoned with these red-hot spices? Ms. Billings and Dr. Sherman had a clue. The two scientists guessed that people who added the spices to their food would have been healthier than those who didn't.

If that guess was right, recipes from tropical climates (where foods spoil faster and the risk of food poisoning is higher) should contain more bacteria-killing spices than those from cool climates. To test their idea, the scientists studied recipes in nearly one hundred cookbooks from all over the world.

First they picked traditional dishes that used meat, since meat spoils quickly.

They chose older recipes that were first used before refrigeration. Collecting more than 4,500 recipes from thirty-six countries, they listed all the spices used.

The bacteria killers were the big winners! Seven of the world's ten most commonly used spices have strong antibacterial power: onion, garlic, hot peppers, bay leaf, cinnamon, cloves, and thyme.

Another finding puzzled the scientists. Pepper and lemon/lime juice ranked second and fifth in the Top Ten. This was surprising because these two spices aren't great at wiping out bacteria. But it turns out that they boost the bacteria-killing power of other spices used with them.

The Spiciest Dishes

What about climate? Did warmer countries have spicier dishes? The scientists compared the average temperature of each country to the number of spices used. They found that dishes from cooler countries had few spices. (In Scandinavia many recipes have no spices at all.)

Foods get spicier as the climate gets hotter. Dishes from tropical countries like Ethiopia, India, and Indonesia used the most spices in the world. They had an average of more than six spices per recipe.

Recipes from hot climates also won the prize for including the most bacteria-killing spices. For example, key ingredients in curry dishes popular in India are cumin, cinnamon, and cloves, all good at killing bacteria or slowing their growth. In the United States, garlic, onion, and hot peppers are used more in the South than they are in the North.

Spices in our food make it more tasty. But as scientists discovered, spices often do an even more important job. People living in hot climates had good reason to get used to strong-tasting spices. These bacteria killers helped preserve foods and kept people healthy.

Today we have other ways to preserve our food, such as refrigerating it and freezing it. But that tasty chili powder might still make your taco a healthier lunch.

Prewriting

Read an article on a topic that interests me. Jot down the 5 W's from the article.

> To get ready to write my summary, I went back through the article and underlined important facts. Then I followed the strategy of making notes on the 5 W's in the article. My underlinings helped me make sure that my 5 W's list didn't leave out any main points.

5 W's

The 5 W's are the **what, who, why, when,** and **where** of an article. Information in these categories provides the substance of the article.

The 5 W's for "What's So Hot About Spices?"

What: the value and use of spices

Who: two scientists studying the use of spices

Why: spices important in food preparation and preservation

When: starting in early times and continuing to the present

Where: the hotter the climate, the more spices used

Go to page 38 in the **Practice the Strategy Notebook!**

Prewriting

Organize   Make a main-idea table.

" My teacher said my summary should be only two or three paragraphs, so I used the strategy of creating a main-idea table for each paragraph.

"Studying my 5 W's notes carefully helped me come up with two main-idea statements and important details that supported them. My 'why' and 'when' notes led me to the first main idea. The second main idea came from my 'who,' 'what,' and 'where' notes. "

Main-Idea Table

A **main-idea table** shows how a main idea is supported by details.

Main Idea
People have always known that spices were important to preserve food.

Detail	Detail	Detail	Detail
Early people traveled to find spices.	Spices keep food from spoiling.	Early people didn't know how spices worked.	Scientists later found that chemicals keep bacteria from growing.

Main Idea
Scientists wondered if eating spicy food in hot climates made people healthier.

Detail	Detail	Detail	Detail
Scientists compared climates and number of spices used.	They found that people in hot climates used more spices.	Most bacteria-killing spices also used in hot climates.	Conclusion: People use spices and stay healthy.

Go to page 41 in the **Practice** the Strategy **Notebook!**

Drafting

Write

Draft my summary. Keep it short, and make sure I present main ideas accurately.

" When I drafted my summary, I really took my time. I looked at my main idea tables and read through the details. This helped me think about the paragraphs I would write. I started by jotting down the topic sentence and then the supporting details for each paragraph. This was easy because I followed my main-idea table.

"I also looked back at the article. I knew from the **Rubric** that it's important to present information accurately. I made sure I wrote only about what the article said and not what I thought about it. Because my summary had to be short and clear, I made sure that all my information tied together in a logical manner.

"When I drafted, I concentrated on getting my ideas down. I did the best I could with spelling and grammar, but I didn't worry too much about them. I knew I could check for errors later. "

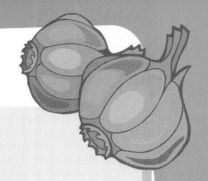

[1st DRAFT]

"What's So Hot About Spices?"

By Gail Jarrow and Paul Sherman

People have always known that spices were important to perserve food. Routes to Asia, where they could find the spices they wanted, were actually being looked for by many early explorers. These included the Phoenicians and Arabs and even Christopher Columbus. Early people didn't know how spices worked. Now we know that chemicles in it keep bacteria from growing in food.

Two scienctists tried to figure out if eating spicy food in hot countries made early peoples healthier. Recipes that were used in different climates before refrigeration were studied by them. They looked at curry recipes and recipes for meat dishes. For each recipe, they also listed it's spices. they found that people in hot climates—where foods spoil more quickly—used more spices. They also used the most bacteria-killing spices. Onion, garlic, hot peppers, and cloves were just a few of the spices people used. For both early peoples and we, spices could add to better health.

Go to page 43 in the **Practice** the Strategy **Notebook!**

Revising

Elaborate

Check to see that I have stayed focused on my topic and not included information that is too detailed.

> After I wrote my first draft, I read it to my partner, Jeannette. She checked my summary against the **Rubric** and thought I had stayed on the topic very well. But she noticed that in two places I had put in information that was too detailed for a summary. I'll go back and take that information out.

READ TO A PARTNER

[2nd DRAFT]

too much detail

People have always known that spices were important to perserve food. Routes to Asia, where they could find the spices they wanted, were actually being looked for by many early explorers. These included the Phoenicians and Arabs and even Christopher Columbus. Early people didn't know how spices worked. Now we know that chemicles in it keep bacteria from growing in food.

too much detail

Two scienctists tried to figure out if eating spicy food in hot countries made early peoples healthier. Recipes that were used in different climates before refrigeration were studied by them. They looked at curry recipes and recipes for meat dishes. For each recipe, they also listed it's spices. they found that people in hot climates—where foods spoil more quickly—used more spices. They also used the most bacteria-killing spices. Onion, garlic, hot peppers, and cloves were just a few of the spices people used. For both early peoples and we, spices could add to better health.

Go to page 45 in the **Practice the Strategy Notebook!**

Revising

Clarify
Make sure I have used active voice as much as possible.

66 The **Rubric** tells me to use active voice as often as I can. Jeannette pointed out a few sentences that would sound a lot clearer in active voice. I rewrote those sentences to make them stronger and more natural. 99

Active Voice, Passive Voice

Active voice tells about the verb. A verb is in active voice if the subject is doing the action in the sentence. Active voice makes your writing stronger.

George **ate** his lunch.

Passive voice also tells about the verb. A verb is in passive voice if the subject is not doing the action in the sentence. Using too many passive verbs weakens your writing.

The lunch **was eaten** by George.

added active voice → **[3rd DRAFT]**

People have always known that spices were important to perserve food. Many early explorers actually were looking for Routes to Asia, where they could find the spices they wanted. were actually being looked for by many early explorers. Early people didn't know how spices worked. Now we know that chemicles in it keep bacteria from growing in food.
— deleted passive voice

Two scienctists tried to figure out if eating spicy food in hot countries made early peoples healthier. They studied ← **added active voice** Recipes that were used in different climates before refrigeration were studied by them. For each recipe, they also — deleted passive voice listed it's spices. they found that people in hot climates—where foods spoil more quickly—used more spices. They also used the most bacteria-killing spices. Onion, garlic, hot peppers, and cloves were just a few of the spices people used. For both early peoples and we, spices could add to better health.

Go to page 46 in the **Practice the Strategy Notebook!**

Editing

Proofread

Check to see that pronouns are used correctly and that all antecedents are clear.

" Now I need to look for errors in my summary. I always check for grammar mistakes and misspelled words. But according to the **Rubric**, I should also make sure I've used pronouns correctly. I need to see that I've used the right forms and didn't make any mistakes with antecedents. "

Pronouns

The pronouns *I, we, you, he, she, it,* and *they* are used as subjects. They are called **subject pronouns**.

> **Subject of sentence:** Irv and **I** are very interested in spicy foods.
>
> **Subject of clause:** Irv decided that **we** should test some samples.

The pronouns *me, us, you, him, her, it,* and *them* are used as objects following verbs and as objects of prepositions. They are called **object pronouns**.

> **Object of verb:** A researcher asked Irv and **me** about the best spicy dishes.
>
> **Object of preposition:** There are free samples of hot sauce for **you** and **him**.

The pronouns *my, mine, our, ours, your, yours, his, hers, its, their,* and *theirs* show possession. They are called **possessive pronouns**. Unlike possessive nouns, they do not use apostrophes.

> Those bottles of hot sauce are **mine; theirs** are the ones on the table.

A pronoun should have a clear **antecedent,** or noun that it refers to. The pronoun must agree with its antecedent in number and gender.

> Irv did not take **his** bottles of hot sauce because **he** had nothing to carry **them** in. (The antecedent of *his* and *he* is *Irv;* the antecedent of *them* is *bottles.*)

Extra Practice

See **Pronouns** (pages CS 8–CS 9) in the back of this book.

Proofreading Marks

⌐ Indent.	ℓ Take out something.
≡ Make a capital.	⊙ Add a period.
/ Make a small letter.	⌗ New paragraph
∧ Add something.	ⓈⓅ Spelling error

[4th DRAFT]

"What's So Hot About Spices?"

by Gail Jarrow and Paul Sherman

People have always known that spices were important to ~~perserve~~ ⓈⓅ preserve food. Many early explorers actually were looking for routes to Asia, where they could find the spices they wanted. Early people didn't know how spices worked. Now we know that ~~chemicles~~ ⓈⓅ chemicals in ~~it~~ them keep bacteria from growing in food. *— agreement with antecedent*

Two ~~scientists~~ scientists tried to figure out if eating spicy food in hot countries made early peoples healthier. They studied recipes that were used in different climates before refrigeration. For each recipe, they also listed ~~it's~~ its spices. ~~they~~ They found that people in hot climates—where foods spoil more quickly—used more spices, ~~They~~ those people also used the most bacteria-killing spices. *not only* *possessive pronoun* *unclear antecedent* Onion, garlic, hot peppers, and cloves were just a few of the spices people used. For both early peoples and ~~we~~ us, spices could add to better health. *object of preposition*

Go to page 47 in the **Practice** the Strategy **Notebook!**

Publishing

Share   Include my summary in a class newsmagazine.

Writer: Paul

Assignment: summary

Topic: spices in food

Audience: classmates and other interested readers

Method of Publication: class newsmagazine

Reason for Choice: I thought the article about spices was so interesting that I wanted to share its information with other people.

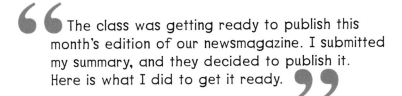

> The class was getting ready to publish this month's edition of our newsmagazine. I submitted my summary, and they decided to publish it. Here is what I did to get it ready.

1. I checked my summary to make sure I had corrected all errors.
2. I typed it up neatly, using a spell checker to catch any typos.
3. I put "Summary by Paul B." at the top of the summary.
4. I found photos of garlic and hot red peppers. I wrote captions and added them to my paper.

"What's So Hot About Spices?"
by Gail Jarrow and Paul Sherman
Summary by Paul B.

People have always known that spices were important to preserve food. Many early explorers actually were looking for routes to Asia, where they could find the spices they wanted. Early people didn't know how spices worked. Now we know that chemicals in them keep bacteria from growing in food.

Two scientists tried to figure out if eating spicy food in hot countries made early peoples healthier. They studied recipes that were used in different climates before refrigeration. For each recipe, they also listed its spices. They found that people in hot climates—where foods spoil more quickly—not only used more spices, but also used the most bacteria-killing spices. Onions, garlic, hot peppers, and cloves were just a few of the spices people used. For both early peoples and us, spices could add to better health.

Hot red peppers

Garlic

USING the Rubric for Assessment

Go to pages 48–49 in the **Practice** the Strategy **Notebook!** Use that rubric to assess Paul's summary. Try using the rubric to assess your own writing.

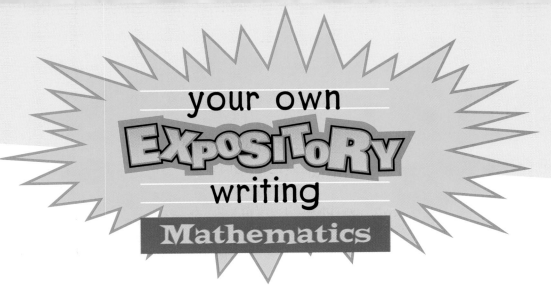

your own EXPOSITORY writing
Mathematics

Put the strategies you practiced in this unit to work to write your own e-mail, summary, or both! You can:

- develop the writing you did in the Your Own Writing pages of the *Practice the Strategy Notebook*;
- pick an idea below and write something new;
- choose another idea of your own.

Be sure to follow the steps in the writing process. Use the rubrics in this unit to assess your writing.

E-Mail

- a question to a math help site about a concept you are having trouble with
- questions to a financial assistance site about how to save and budget money
- questions to a math game site about new math games and puzzles

Summary

Find an article on one of these topics and write a summary of it:
- how people wrote numbers before they knew about zero
- Carl Friedrich Gauss, a mathematical genius who could add 100 numbers in minutes
- how we got leap years

portfolio

School–Home Connection

Keep a writing portfolio. Think about adding the activities from the *Practice the Strategy Notebook* to your writing portfolio. You may want to take your portfolio home to share.

DESCRIPTIVE

writing

provides clear word pictures of
objects, people, places, or events.

1

Descriptive Essay

2

Observation Report

DESCRIPTIVE writing

Descriptive Essay

In this chapter, you will have a chance to do one kind of descriptive writing, a **descriptive essay**.

A **descriptive essay** gives, in words, a clear, detailed picture of a specific person, place, thing, or event. The descriptive essay in this chapter will focus on a place.

The piece of writing on the next page is a descriptive essay of a place. Read these questions. Then read the essay. Keep the questions in mind as you read.

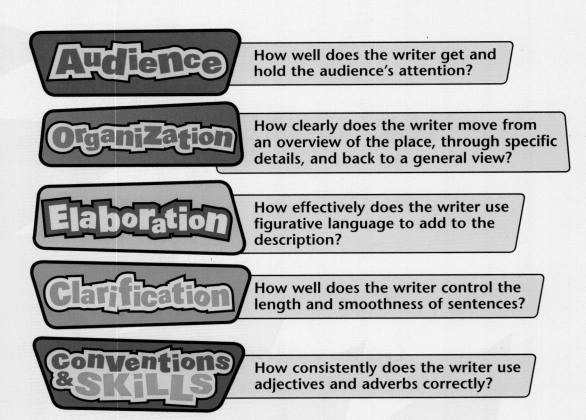

Audience
How well does the writer get and hold the audience's attention?

Organization
How clearly does the writer move from an overview of the place, through specific details, and back to a general view?

Elaboration
How effectively does the writer use figurative language to add to the description?

Clarification
How well does the writer control the length and smoothness of sentences?

Conventions & Skills
How consistently does the writer use adjectives and adverbs correctly?

A Visit to the Past

by Timothy O'Malley

In August of A.D. 79, life ended for the Italian city of Pompeii. Mount Vesuvius, a volcano just to the north, exploded with violent force. Most of the city's citizens escaped, but some refused to leave their homes. Everyone who stayed behind was either asphyxiated by poisonous gases or buried alive under pumice, ash, and other materials. Buried in more than 15 feet of volcanic debris, Pompeii remained untouched for centuries. Excavations have now uncovered the remains of a city that was literally stopped dead in its tracks.

In Pompeii today, it is possible to see evidence of the citizens' everyday life and of the sudden, terrible death of many. The remains help to paint a picture of the city as it was when time stood still on that August day.

The Forum is where major religious and government events took place. Much of it is still standing. Several two-story marble columns that marked off the open meeting area remain. They hover like sentinels standing guard. Nearby are half-destroyed temples and other buildings. East of the city lies the amphitheater. Grass covers much of it now with a soft green blanket. But it is easy to imagine audiences shouting and applauding as they watched gladiators perform here.

Stores and businesses are on many of the streets. These provide a close look at where citizens bought and sold their wares. Baked goods, fine woven cloth, and drinking vessels were just a few of the items that citizens could buy. Some of the stores stood separate from other buildings. Others were tucked into corners of larger homes. Still others were storefronts, with families living behind them.

One fascinating aspect of Pompeii is the large number of private houses. Nowhere else is it possible to see such a wide range of structures from so many time periods. One structure is called the House of the Faun. It fills a full city block. Its walls feature beautiful mosaics and murals. Other large homes feature elaborate, pillared entrances. Most are decorated with floor mosaics worked into detailed patterns. Such houses generally enclose lovely courtyards and gardens.

The excavations of the buildings and streets of Pompeii show a well-off, bustling city. Other remains show just how quickly the volcano did its work. Many human remains were found. Covered with layers of smoothed-down molten ash, the bodies look like sculptures made of soft clay. Many were found in completely natural positions. They probably never knew what hit them.

A site like Pompeii can show us many things. It can show how citizens of ancient Roman cities lived and worked. It can show us their art and culture. It also points out very clearly how overwhelming natural forces can be. There are indeed many lessons to learn from Pompeii.

Using a Rubric

A rubric is a tool that lists "what counts" for a piece of writing.

How does a rubric work? You assign 1, 2, 3, or 4 points to qualities in a piece of writing to show how well the author dealt with them. The questions on page 104 were used to make this rubric.

> Let me introduce myself. I'm Inez, and I'm learning how to write a descriptive essay, too. What did you think of the descriptive essay you just read? Read this rubric. Start with the questions. Then read the information that goes with each question. We'll use the rubric to evaluate the essay.

Audience

How well does the writer get and hold the audience's attention?

Organization

How clearly does the writer move from an overview of the place, through specific details, and back to a general view?

Elaboration

How effectively does the writer use figurative language to add to the description?

Clarification

How well does the writer control the length and smoothness of sentences?

Conventions & Skills

How consistently does the writer use adjectives and adverbs correctly?

Score 1 Point
(Novice)

The topic is not clearly identified and sustained.

The paper lacks organization, so it is hard to know where the writer is going with it.

No attempts are made at using figurative language.

Sentences vary wildly in length, and relationships among ideas are unclear.

Adverbs and adjectives are consistently used incorrectly.

Score 2 Points
(Apprentice)

The topic is introduced, but details that follow do not always clearly relate to it.

Specific and general details are sometimes mixed together inappropriately.

Some similes and metaphors are used, but they do not always fit well with the topic.

Some sentences are good, but many are long and confusing or short and choppy.

Some adjectives and adverbs are used correctly, but there are several mistakes.

Score 3 Points
(Proficient)

The topic is clearly introduced, and most details are chosen to interest the audience.

For the most part, the paper moves from the general to the specific and back to the general.

A number of appropriate similes and metaphors are used.

Most sentences read smoothly and show good combination of ideas.

There are a few mistakes with adjectives and adverbs.

Score 4 Points
(Distinguished)

The introduction is fresh and descriptive details keep the reader engaged.

The paper moves smoothly from the general to the specific and back to the general.

Similes and metaphors add freshness and originality to descriptions.

Ideas are combined effectively in clear, well-constructed sentences.

There are no mistakes with adjectives and adverbs.

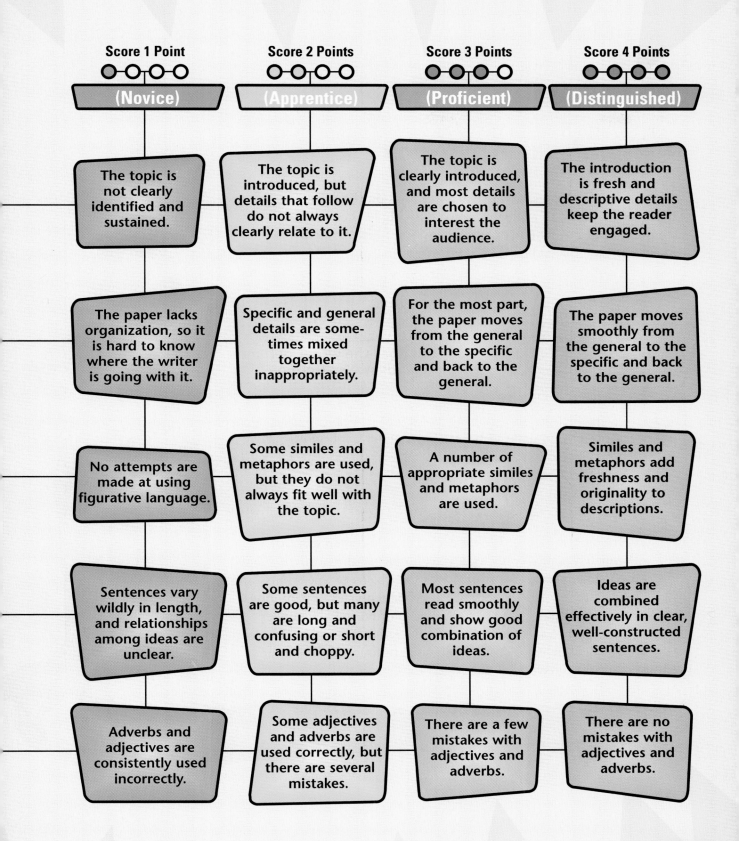

Using a Rubric to Study the Model

With your classmates, discuss each question on the rubric. Then use the rubric to evaluate Timothy O'Malley's essay on each question. Find sentences and paragraphs in it that help you answer each question.

Audience

How well does the writer get and hold the audience's attention?

" The writer really got my attention with his opening sentence about life ending. Then he told me just enough about Pompeii in his first paragraph that I wanted to find out what it looks like now. Read what he wrote. "

In August of A.D. 79, life ended for the Italian city of Pompeii. Mount Vesuvius, a volcano just to the north, exploded with violent force. Most of the city's citizens escaped, but some refused to leave their homes. Everyone who stayed behind was either asphyxiated by poisonous gases or buried alive under pumice, ash, and other materials. Buried in more than 15 feet of volcanic debris, Pompeii remained untouched for centuries. Excavations have now uncovered the remains of a city that was literally stopped dead in its tracks.

How clearly does the writer move from an overview of the place, through specific details, and back to a general view?

" After introducing the topic at the beginning of the paper, the writer gives a lot of specific descriptions in the next few paragraphs. At the end, he sort of stands back so he can summarize all the things he's described. "

A site like Pompeii can show us many things. It can show how citizens of ancient Roman cities lived and worked. It can show us their art and culture. It also points out very clearly how overwhelming natural forces can be. There are indeed many lessons to learn from Pompeii.

How effectively does the writer use figurative language to add to the description?

" The writer uses some figurative expressions that I've heard before, like "time stood still," but they really seem to fit with this topic. He also uses some original similes and metaphors, such as the underlined ones in this paragraph. "

Several two-story marble columns that marked off the open meeting area remain. They <u>hover like sentinels</u> standing guard. Nearby are half-destroyed temples and other buildings. East of the city lies the amphitheater. Grass covers much of it now <u>with a soft green blanket.</u>

Clarification

How well does the writer control the length and smoothness of sentences?

66 I can see that the writer did a good job of combining ideas using compound verbs and objects. But he was careful not to let his sentences get too long or confusing. All the sentences read smoothly. 99

Its walls feature beautiful mosaics and murals. Other large homes feature elaborate, pillared entrances. Most are decorated with floor mosaics worked into detailed patterns. Such houses generally enclose lovely courtyards and gardens.

Conventions & Skills

How consistently does the writer use adjectives and adverbs correctly?

66 The writer knew how to use adjectives and adverbs correctly. Here are a few examples. 99

Some of the stores stood separate from other buildings.

Other remains show just how quickly the volcano did its work.

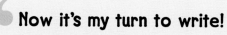

66 **Now it's my turn to write!**

I'm going to write my own descriptive essay. Watch me as I use the model and also the rubric to practice good writing strategies. 99

Inez

Writer of a Descriptive Essay

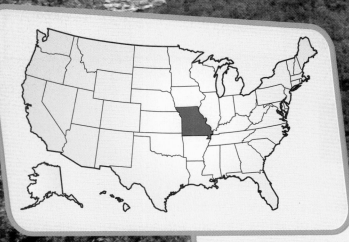

Name:	Inez
Home:	Missouri
Hobbies:	collecting stamps from other countries, learning about the weather
Favorite Book:	*The Talking Earth* by Jean Craighead George
Favorite Teacher:	Mrs. Dudzek, my science teacher
Assignment:	descriptive essay

Prewriting

Gather

Use an atlas to find a place to describe. Then research the place in three other appropriate sources.

" I went to the atlas to choose a place for my topic, but I didn't have to look long. It's been so hot here that I wanted to write about somewhere entirely different. So I chose Antarctica! "

Atlas

An **atlas** is a book that contains maps and geographical information based on them.

" The atlas showed me the location of Antarctica and gave information about its terrain. When we talk about places in my social studies class, though, we always include topics like climate, animals that live there, the people who live there, and other things. I knew my audience would want to know about those things in Antarctica. I went to other sources for more information. "

Prewriting

Gather

Use an atlas to find a place to describe. Then research the place in three other appropriate sources.

" I came up with a list of questions I thought my audience would want answers for. My questions were:

What does Antarctica look like?

What is the weather like in Antarctica?

What plants and animals live in Antarctica?

Do people live in Antarctica?

"I followed the strategy and chose three sources, besides the atlas, to get more information. It was fun to do research online, but I chose my Internet source carefully. Most Internet sites are good, but some are put together sloppily or offer opinions not supported by facts. "

Appropriate Sources

An **appropriate source** is a place to get information that is suitable, right, or proper for your purpose. Here are some good sources for information about specific places:

- **an encyclopedia:** to get a good overview of the place

- **an almanac:** to get current facts and figures about things like government, population, dimensions of mountains and rivers

- **a travel guidebook:** to learn about specific areas and what to see in them

- **an Internet site:** to get answers to common questions about the place, to see pictures of it

Prewriting

Gather

Use an atlas to find a place to describe. Then research the place in three other appropriate sources.

" The three sources I chose were an encyclopedia, an Internet site, and a recent book about Antarctica that I found in the school library. I jotted down notes from each source that would help me answer my questions. "

Internet Site:

mostly scientists live in Antarctica

they live in science "stations"

   Amundsen-Scott Station—huge geodesic dome

   McMurdo Station—more than 100 buildings

temperatures as low as −128° F

Encyclopedia:

fierce, biting winds

covered with huge sheet of ice

Emperor and Adélie penguins live there

huge birds called skuas live there

Library Book:

East Antarctica—a high, flat plateau

West Antarctica—mountainous islands

often too cold to snow

lichen and mosses grow

Go to page 50 in the Practice the Strategy Notebook!

Descriptive Writing • Descriptive Essay

Prewriting

Organize — Make a web of descriptive details.

"I got a lot of information from my sources, but I needed to make it all work together. My strategy was to use a web to organize the most important descriptive details into categories. My main categories came from my list of questions. They are in the green circles."

Web

A **web** organizes information about one main topic. The main topic goes in the center circle. Related details go in smaller circles connected to the center circle.

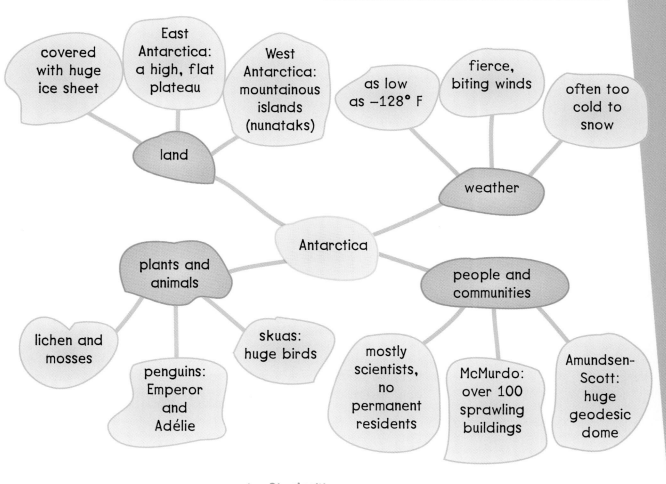

- covered with huge ice sheet
- East Antarctica: a high, flat plateau
- West Antarctica: mountainous islands (nunataks)
- land
- as low as −128° F
- fierce, biting winds
- often too cold to snow
- weather
- Antarctica
- plants and animals
- lichen and mosses
- penguins: Emperor and Adélie
- skuas: huge birds
- people and communities
- mostly scientists, no permanent residents
- McMurdo: over 100 sprawling buildings
- Amundsen-Scott: huge geodesic dome

Go to page 52 in the Practice the Strategy Notebook!

Descriptive Writing • Descriptive Essay

115

Drafting

Write

Draft my descriptive essay. Move from a general introduction to specific details and back to a general conclusion.

" The **Rubric** tells me to get the audience's attention and then keep it. I figured a strong introduction, followed by well-organized details, would help me do both those things. When I draft my paper, I'll use my web to keep me on track. I'll write a paragraph about each of my main points. Then I'll tie everything together in my conclusion.

"When I draft, I'll concentrate on getting my ideas down and not worry about catching mistakes. I'll have time to fix things later. "

Introduction, Conclusion

The **introduction** is the first paragraph of a paper. A good introduction grabs the audience's attention and states the main idea of the paper.

> In a descriptive essay, use the introductory paragraph to give general information or background about your place.

The **conclusion** is the last paragraph of a longer paper. The conclusion ties up loose ends and summarizes main points.

> In a descriptive essay, use the conclusion to summarize, but also to refer back to the introduction. The conclusion may also restate information that was presented in the introduction.

Descriptive Writing • Descriptive Essay

introduction

[1st DRAFT]

A White World

"Everywhere you look, all you see is white." ~~These words~~ This is how many travelers to Antarctica explain their reaction to this isolated continent. Antarctica is not a place where most people would want to live. However, to many visitors it appears quite remarkably.

Antarctica is covered almost complete with a huge ice sheet. It extends almost five and a half million square miles and the thickly part averages about 6,500 feet. The land is divided into sections. East Antarctica is a high, flat platou. West Antarctica is smallest. It is a series of mountainus islands held together by the ice sheet. In some areas are nunataks. Nunataks are mountains buried so deep that only their tips peek through the ice. Between East and West Antarctica are the Transantarctic mountains. They cut the land into two neat chunks. On either side of West Antarctica are ~~big~~ huge floating ice sheets. One, the Ross Ice Shelf, is as large as France.

details about the land

Descriptive Writing · Descriptive Essay

117

details
about
weather

The weather in Antarctica is real cold. In the winter tempertures drop as low as –128 degrees Fahrenheit. The average winter range is from –40 to –94 degrees inland. These temperatures can freeze spit in midair. You have to take them serious. Winds are fierce and biting. Gusts over 100 miles per hour are not uncommon. Even in summer, in warmer coastal areas, +32 degrees is the average temperture. But no snow falls in many parts of Antarctica. Strong winds kick up exsisting snow, but the air is usually so dry that new snow cannot form. This is why Antarctica is sometimes called "The white Desert."

details
about
plants
and
animals

Plants and animals are more commonlier in Antarctica than you might expect. There are several hundred species of lichens. They grow good along the rocks and they create colorful colonies of yellow, green, and black. Mosses can also be found. The main animals living in Antarctica are penguins, of which the emperor penguin, about three or four feet tall, scoots around the ice like an industrious headwaiter, and the Adélie, slightly smaller, also lives in large colonies. The South Polar skua is a huge and powerful flying bird. It has been seen as far inland as the Pole. It has also been seen as far north as the Equator.

Surprisingly, people also live in Antarctica. Nearly all of them are scientists. (No one, though, makes this cold continent a permanent home.) Including the United States, 29 countries have research stations. The largest is the American facility called McMurdo Station. It is on Ross Island in the Ross Ice Shelf. This community contains about 100 low, sprawling buildings. There are dormitories, a gymnasium, a science lab, and other structures. About 250 people spend the winter there. In summer the population rises to 1,000. A smaller facility is the Amundsen-Scott South Pole Station. It is very close to the Pole. The main building is a huge aluminum geodesic dome. It is more than 55 feet high at its highest point. Housing space for 27 people, equipment depots, and various research areas are either within it or connected to it by covered passageways. Glinting in the sun in the empty Antarctic plain, the station looks like the home of visitors from another planet.

details about people

Tourists do visit Antarctica. However, it can cost as much as $40,000 to get all the way to the South Pole. If you have the money, and are adventurous enough to make the trip, you can visit this unique isolated continent.

conclusion

Go to page 54 in the **Practice** the Strategy **Notebook!**

Revising

Elaborate
Look for places to insert figurative language, including similes and metaphors.

READ TO A PARTNER

" I read my first draft to my partner, Tamika. She liked most of my descriptive details, but she said that my description of the land itself was kind of dull. I went back and added figurative language, including some similes and metaphors. "

Figurative Language

Figurative language is language that goes beyond the normal meaning of the words in it. Figurative language creates a mental picture for the reader.

A **simile** compares two different things by using the words *like* or *as*.

> The icy rain cut through the air **like tiny daggers**.

A **metaphor** compares two different things by calling one thing another.

> The **edge** of the glacier **was** a long, smooth **slide** for the penguins.

[2nd DRAFT]

Antarctica is covered almost complete with a huge ice sheet. It extends almost five and a half million square miles and the thickly part averages about 6,500 feet. The land is divided into sections. East Antarctica is

metaphor ——————→ —an icy table of land

a high, flat platou. West Antarctica is smallest. It is a series of

mountainus islands held together by the ice sheet. In some areas ~~are~~

simile ——————→ dot the surface like punctuation marks

nunataks. Nunataks are mountains buried so deep that only their tips peek through the ice. Between East and West Antarctica are the Transantarctic mountains. They cut the land into two neat chunks. On

that hug the land like armrests on a chair

either side of West Antarctica are huge floating ice sheets. One, the

Ross Ice Shelf, is as large as France. simile ⌐

Go to page 56 in the **Practice** the Strategy **Notebook!**

Descriptive Writing • Descriptive Essay

Revising

Clarify
Combine short, choppy sentences.
Rewrite long, confusing sentences.

" Tamika also commented on some of my sentences. She noticed that some were really short, but a few were so long that it was hard to understand them. The way I fixed one of my paragraphs was to combine two or three short sentences if they were about the same subject. But if two or three ideas were combined into a sentence that got confusing, then I broke that sentence apart. "

[3rd DRAFT]

combined sentences

Plants and animals are more commonlier in Antarctica than you might expect. There are several hundred species of lichens, They grow good along the rocks, and they create colorful colonies of yellow, green, and black. Mosses can also be found. The main animals living in Antarctica are penguins, of which the emperor penguin, about three or four feet tall, scoots around the ice like an industrious headwaiter, and the Adélie, slightly smaller, also lives in large colonies. The South Polar skua

rewrote long sentence

there

is a huge and powerful flying bird. It has been seen as far inland as the Pole, It has also been seen as far north as the Equator.

and

combined sentences

Go to page 57 in the **Practice the Strategy Notebook!**

Descriptive Writing · Descriptive Essay

Editing

Proofread

Check to see that adjectives and adverbs are used correctly.

" Now I need to look for errors in my essay. I always make sure I don't have any capitalization or spelling errors. But the **Rubric** also tells me to check for mistakes with adjectives and adverbs. I know that sometimes it's easy to get the two mixed up. "

Adjectives, Adverbs

An **adjective** is a word that describes a noun or pronoun. An adjective tells which one, what kind, or how many. It usually comes before the word it describes. It may also follow a linking verb such as *is, feels, sounds, becomes, seems, looks,* or *appears.*

> The ice sheet looks **barren** to **some** people, but it seems **beautiful** to others.

An **adverb** is a word that describes a verb, an adjective, or another adverb. An adverb tells how, when, where, or to what extent. Some adverbs end in *–ly,* but many common ones, such as *now, again, here,* and *soon,* do not.

> **Sometimes** storms arise **very quickly,** and you would do **well** to avoid them.

Comparative adjectives and adverbs compare two things. They are formed with the ending *–er* or with *more.* **Superlative** adjectives and adverbs compare more than two things. They are formed with the ending *–est* or with *most.*

Adjectives	Adverbs
colder than yesterday	**more frequently** than before
coldest day in the last week	**most frequently** of all

Extra Practice
See **Adjectives, Adverbs** (pages CS 10-CS 11) in the back of this book.

Proofreading Marks

⌐ Indent.

≡ Make a capital.

∕ Make a small letter.

∧ Add something.

ℓ Take out something.

⊙ Add a period.

⌗ New paragraph

(SP) Spelling error

[4th DRAFT]

A White World

"Everywhere you look, all you see is white." This is how many travelers to Antarctica explain their reaction to this isolated continent. Antarctica is not a place where most people would want to live. However, to many visitors it appears quite remarkably. *remarkable* — adjective after linking verb

adverb modifying action verb —

Antarctica is covered almost complete *completely* with a huge ice sheet. *adjective modifying noun* — a It extends almost five and a half million square miles and the thickly *thickest* part averages about 6,500 feet. The land is divided into sections. East Antarctica is a high, flat plateu *(SP) plateau* —an icy table of land. *comparative adjective →* West Antarctica is smallest *smaller*. It is a series of mountainus *(SP) mountainous* islands held together by the ice sheet. In some areas nunataks dot the surface like punctuation marks. Nunataks are mountains buried so deep that only their tips peek through the ice. Between East and West Antarctica are the Transantarctic mountains. They cut the land into two neat chunks. On either side of West Antarctica are huge floating ice sheets that hug the land like armrests on a chair. One, the Ross Ice Shelf, is as large as France.

adverb modifying adjective —

The weather in Antarctica is real *ly* cold. In the winter temperatures *(SP) temperatures* drop as low as −128 degrees Fahrenheit. The average winter range is

adverb modifying verb —

from −40 to −94 degrees inland. These temperatures *(SP) temperatures* can freeze spit in midair. You have to take them serious *ly*. Winds are fierce and biting. Gusts over 100 miles per hour are not uncommon. Even in summer, in warmer coastal areas, +32 degrees is the average temperture *(SP) temperature*. But no snow falls in many parts of Antarctica. Strong winds kick up exsisting *(SP) existing* snow, but the air is usually so dry that new snow cannot form.

Go to page 59 in the **Practice** ∧*the Strategy* **Notebook!**

Publishing

Share

Display my essay on a "Where in the World?" bulletin board.

Writer:	Inez
Assignment:	descriptive essay
Topic:	Antarctica
Audience:	classmates and others viewing our display
Method of Publication:	class bulletin board
Reason for Choice:	Antarctica is a great "Where in the World?" topic.

" I thought my descriptive essay about Antarctica would be an unusual contribution to our class's 'Where in the World?' bulletin board display. Here's what I did to get it ready. "

1. I checked my essay one more time to be sure it was as good as I could make it.

2. I found a map and pictures of things and places I described on the Internet. I printed them out and pasted them onto construction paper.

3. I pasted my essay onto other sheets of construction paper.

4. I mounted my essay and pictures on the bulletin board.

Descriptive Writing • Descriptive Essay

A White World
by Inez

"Everywhere you look, all you see is white." This is how many travelers to Antarctica explain their reaction to this isolated continent. Antarctica is not a place where most people would want to live. However, to many visitors it appears quite remarkable.

Antarctica is covered almost completely with a huge ice sheet. It extends almost five and a half million square miles and the thickest part averages about 6,500 feet. The land is divided into sections. East Antarctica is a high, flat plateau—an icy table of land. West Antarctica is smaller. It is a series of mountainous islands held together by the ice sheet. In some areas, nunataks dot the surface like punctuation marks. Nunataks are mountains buried so deep that only their tips peek through the ice. Between East and West Antarctica are the Transantarctic Mountains. They cut the land into two neat chunks. On either side of West Antarctica are huge floating ice sheets that hug the land like armrests on a chair. One, the Ross Ice Shelf, is as large as France.

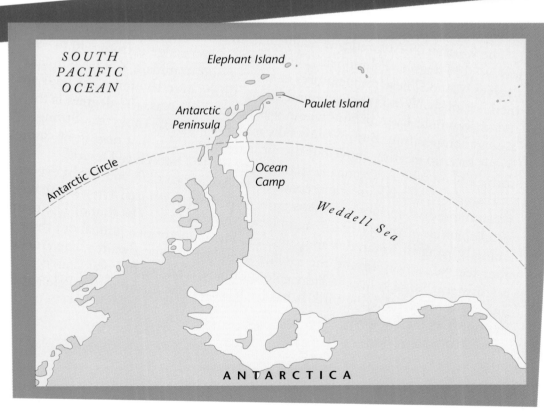

SOUTH PACIFIC OCEAN

Elephant Island

Paulet Island

Antarctic Peninsula

Antarctic Circle

Ocean Camp

Weddell Sea

ANTARCTICA

The weather in Antarctica is really cold. In the winter, temperatures drop as low as −128 degrees Fahrenheit. The average winter range is from −40 to −94 degrees inland. These temperatures can freeze spit in midair. You have to take them seriously. Winds are fierce and biting. Gusts over 100 miles per hour are not uncommon. Even in summer, in warmer coastal areas, +32 degrees is the average temperature. But no snow falls in many parts of Antarctica. Strong winds kick up existing snow, but the air is usually so dry that new snow cannot form. This is why Antarctica is sometimes called "The White Desert."

Plants and animals are more common in Antarctica than you might expect. Several hundred species of lichens grow well along the rocks. They create colorful colonies of yellow, green, and black. Mosses can also be found. The main animals living in Antarctica are penguins. The emperor penguin, about three or four feet tall, scoots around the ice like an industrious headwaiter. The Adélie, slightly smaller, also lives in large colonies there. The South Polar skua is a huge and powerful flying bird. It has been seen as far inland as the Pole and as far north as the Equator.

Surprisingly, people also live in Antarctica. Nearly all of them are scientists. (No one, though, makes this cold, forbidding region a permanent home.) Including the United States, 29 countries have research stations. The largest is the American facility called McMurdo Station. It is on Ross Island in the Ross Ice Shelf. This community contains about 100 low, sprawling buildings. There are dormitories, a gymnasium, a science lab, and other structures. About 250 people spend the winter there. In summer the population rises to 1,000. A smaller facility is the Amundsen-Scott South Pole Station. It is very close to the Pole. The main building is a huge aluminum geodesic dome. It is more than 55 feet high at its highest point. Housing space for 27 people, equipment depots, and various research areas are either within it or connected to it by covered passageways. Glinting in the sun in the empty Antarctic plain, the station looks like the home of visitors from another planet.

Tourists do visit Antarctica. However, it can cost as much as $40,000 to get all the way to the South Pole. If you have the money, and are adventurous enough to make the trip, you can visit this unique isolated continent.

USING the Rubric for Assessment

Go to pages 60-61 of your **Practice the Strategy Notebook!** Use that rubric to assess Inez's paper. Try using the rubric to assess your own writing.

DESCRIPTIVE
writing

Observation Report

This chapter will give you an opportunity to do one kind of descriptive writing, an **observation report**.

An **observation report** describes an object, person, event, or process in vivid detail. It is an eyewitness account that emphasizes descriptive detail.

The piece of writing on the next page is an observation report. First, read the questions below. Then read the report, keeping the questions in mind as you read.

 How clearly does the writer present word pictures that help the audience experience what the writer observed?

 How well are main ideas organized into paragraphs with a clear focus and strong descriptive details?

 How effectively has the writer chosen and included appropriate pictures to give more depth and meaning to verbal descriptions?

 How well has the writer kept the description lively by varying sentence length and pattern?

 How consistently has the writer used correct subject-verb agreement?

OBSERVATIONS OF A BIRD WATCHER

by Naomi Greenberg

An outdoor bird feeder can be fun to observe any time of year. Watching the one in my backyard for just a few months gave me a real education in bird behavior.

Cardinals, for example, are not only beautiful; they are also very clever. The all-red, crested male approaches the feeder on his own and checks out the territory. When he has made sure no enemies (that is, cats) are nearby, he leaves, and then the female, more brown than red, arrives to feed at her leisure. Mr. Cardinal still keeps watch, though, from a nearby branch. Later, he and his mate may perch together in an out-of-the-way spot, with the male transferring tasty tidbits from his beak to hers. At such moments the two may "cheep" softly to each other. At other times, though, their call may be loud, almost strident.

Other loud birds around the feeder are the blue jays. These crested fellows are good looking, but have very poor manners, pushing smaller birds away in their eagerness to eat. Only recently did I realize that some of the jay's noisiness has a purpose. Listening to the bird's loud, repeated "jay, jay" call one day, it occurred to me that it sounded like a warning siren. I looked out at the feeder, and sure enough, a cat was stalking nearby.

Besides the beautiful cardinals and jays, several more ordinary-looking birds often crowd around the feeder. Flocks of gray-brown sparrows usually arrive in groups, but politely wait their turn perching on the telephone wire just above the feeder. House finches, sparrowlike birds with a reddish forehead and breast, show the same good manners, chattering to each other as they sit and wait. Mourning doves often pick at seeds that have fallen from the feeder.

During spring migration, new species appear. Tiny, bright yellow goldfinches dropped by one day late last April. But the biggest thrill was the visit of the gorgeous grosbeaks. One or two of the black, white, and gold-colored males came first, in early May, followed the next day by at least ten companions. After a day or two of feeding, the birds lost their bedraggled look and moved on, perhaps to other bird feeders.

Using a Rubric

A rubric is an evaluation tool. It lists "what counts" in a piece of writing.

How do you use a rubric? Remember, you assign 1, 2, 3, or 4 points to qualities in the writing. These points show how well the author dealt with the various qualities.

The questions on page 128 were used to make this rubric.

"Hi! My name is Chris. I'm learning about observation reports, too. What did you think of the report on page 129? Take a look at this rubric. Begin with the questions; then go on to read the assessment information for each question. We'll be using the rubric to evaluate the observation report you just read."

Audience

How clearly does the writer present word pictures that help the audience experience what the writer observed?

Organization

How well are main ideas organized into paragraphs with a clear focus and strong descriptive details?

Elaboration

How effectively has the writer chosen and included appropriate pictures to give more depth and meaning to verbal descriptions?

Clarification

How well has the writer kept the description lively by varying sentence length and pattern?

Conventions & Skills

How consistently has the writer used correct subject-verb agreement?

Score 1 Point
(Novice)

The writer seems unaware that there is an audience for the report.

Ideas run together with no clear order or organization.

The writer includes no pictures.

Sentence patterns are the same throughout, and sentences are all about the same length.

There are many errors with subject-verb agreement.

Score 2 Points
(Apprentice)

There are few word pictures to help readers experience what the writer observed.

Some paragraphs have a clear focus, but there are few descriptive details.

The writer uses pictures, but they do not always tie clearly to the report.

The writer shows some variety in sentence length, but most sentences follow the same pattern.

There are several errors with subject-verb agreement.

Score 3 Points
(Proficient)

Clear word pictures help readers experience what the writer observed through at least one sense.

Most paragraphs have a clear focus and effective descriptive details.

The pictures clearly relate to the descriptions in the report.

The writer varies sentence pattern and length, with only a few unnatural-sounding sentences.

There are a few errors with subject-verb agreement.

Score 4 Points
(Distinguished)

Vivid word pictures help readers experience what the writer observed through several senses.

Each paragraph has a clear focus, and details create a vivid description of the experience.

Pictures clearly relate to descriptions and deepen readers' understanding.

The writer varies sentence pattern and length to create interesting, natural-sounding sentences.

There are no errors with subject-verb agreement.

Using a **Rubric** to Study the Model

Discuss each question on the rubric with your classmates. Then use the rubric to evaluate Naomi Greenberg's observation report. Find sentences and paragraphs in it that help you answer each question.

Audience

How clearly does the writer present word pictures that help the audience experience what the writer observed?

66 I think this writer made her observation experience really come alive for her audience. One way she did this was by telling how the birds sounded as well as how they looked. For example, take another look at how she described the cardinals' behavior. 99

Later, he and his mate may perch together in an out-of-the-way spot, with the male transferring tasty tidbits from his beak to hers. At such moments the two may "cheep" softly to each other. At other times, though, their call may be loud, almost strident.

How well are main ideas organized into paragraphs with a clear focus and strong descriptive details?

" Each paragraph in the body of the report has a clear focus. The writer even began each paragraph with a topic sentence. Sentences within each paragraph then provide clear, descriptive details that support the topic sentences. Look at the careful construction of this paragraph. "

Besides the beautiful cardinals and jays, several more ordinary-looking birds often crowd around the feeder. Flocks of gray-brown sparrows usually arrive in groups, but politely wait their turn perching on the telephone wire just above the feeder. House finches . . . show the same good manners. . . .

How effectively has the writer chosen and included appropriate pictures to give more depth and meaning to verbal descriptions?

" The picture the writer chose helps demonstrate the activities and appearance of the birds. "

Clarification

How well has the writer kept the description lively by varying sentence length and pattern?

" The writer has a nice mix of short and long sentences, and there is variety in their structure. Here are some examples. The first example starts with a prepositional phrase; the second example starts with a dependent clause. "

During spring migration, new species appear.

When he has made sure no enemies (that is, cats) are nearby, he leaves. . . .

Conventions & Skills

How consistently has the writer used correct subject-verb agreement?

" I didn't notice any problems with subject-verb agreement in the report. The following sentences show you how carefully the writer avoided this error. "

Other loud birds around the feeder are the blue jays.

House finches, sparrowlike birds with a reddish forehead and breast, show the same good manners. . . .

" Now it's my turn to write!

I'm going to write an observation report of my own. Watch to see how I use the model and also the rubric to practice good writing strategies. "

Descriptive Writing • Observation Report

ChRiS

Writer of an
Observation Report

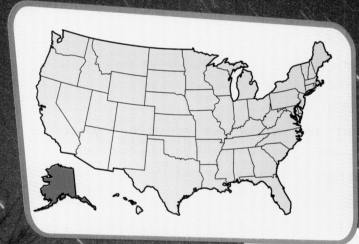

Name:	Chris
Home:	Alaska
Hobbies:	hiking, astronomy
Favorite Book:	*Exploring the Night Sky: The Equinox Astronomy Guide for Beginners* by Terence Dickinson
Favorite Teacher:	Mr. Schneider, my science teacher
Assignment:	observation report

Prewriting

Gather

Choose an aspect of nature to observe. Make notes (with sketches) of what I am observing.

" Last week Mom and I saw the aurora borealis, or northern lights, in the sky above our woods. I decided the lights could be a perfect topic for my observation report.

"Last night I went out, and the show was terrific! To start planning my report, I followed the strategy of making notes of what I observed. I'm no artist, but I drew some sketches to help me remember things. I can find photos to add to my report later. "

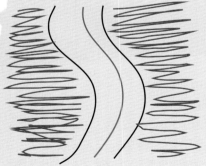

- cold night, crisp breezes, smell of fresh pine
- one arc of light spreads across the sky, followed by several more (white, with red and purple at edges)
- rays of light form "drapes" across the sky, seem to blow softly in the wind (light up whole sky)
- hissing noises as sky lights up
- drapes disappear, and reappear as new rays shoot down from space (white with purple in between)
- after 10–15 minutes drapes start to spread wider, color starts to fade
- lights blink on and off, then disappear

Go to page 62 in the **Practice the Strategy Notebook!**

Prewriting

Organize
Make an observation chart to organize my notes.

❝ To help my audience feel like they were there for the light show, I used the strategy of organizing my experience into an observation chart. That way I'd make sure to convey what was going on through as many senses as possible. Of course, I couldn't smell or hear the aurora borealis, but I could smell and hear other things around me. I decided those things would add to my description, so I put them in my chart. ❞

Observation Chart

An **observation chart** organizes information that has been gathered by using sight, sound, touch, taste, and smell. Appealing to as many senses as possible is a good way to get the reader involved in the experience.

Topic: aurora borealis				
Sight • arcs of white light spread across the sky (red and purple at edges) • rays of light form "drapes" that seem to sway in the wind • drapes disappear, then reappear (mostly white; purple in between) • lights spread thinner, blink on and off, fade out	**Sound** • hissing noises at height of light show	**Touch** • crisp evening breezes	**Taste**	**Smell** • sweet smell of pine trees in the air

Go to page 64 in the Practice the Strategy Notebook!

Drafting

Draft my report. Be sure that each body paragraph has a clear focus with strong descriptive details.

" Once I collected all my information, I got ready to draft my report. I decided to describe the light show in the order that things happened. This wasn't too difficult because I had listed the sights on my observation chart in chronological, or time, order. I knew I could follow that, adding in other sense observations where they belonged.

"The **Rubric** reminded me to make sure my paragraphs have a clear focus and descriptive details. I decided to have a new paragraph in the body of the paper every time the lights changed shape. I also thought it might be a good idea to use topic sentences when I could.

"When I drafted, I worried mainly about getting my ideas down. I figured I could check for errors later. "

Body

The **body** is the main part of your writing. The body follows the introduction and develops your main ideas.

Topic Sentence, Detail Sentence

The **topic sentence** states or contains the main idea of a paragraph. While it is often the first sentence in the paragraph, it may also be positioned in the middle or at the end of the paragraph.

A **detail sentence** supports the paragraph's main idea. The detail sentences in one paragraph should go with, tell about, or describe the main idea.

Observing the Aurora Borealis, or Northern Lights

Sometimes I'm really happy that we live so far north. This is the reason. If you are lucky, on certin nights you may see the aurora borealis, or northern lights. Here is ~~what I saw~~ my observation from a night last week when the lights appeared:

topic sentence

It is a perfect night ~~for~~ for a light show. The air feels crisp and cold as a gentle breeze touches my skin. I can smell the fresh pine trees growing in the nearby woods. Stars are twinkeling.

detail sentences

I watch the sky. A great white arc of light begin to appear. It stretches larger and larger. Several more follow it. They expand. They become red and purple, especially at the edges.

body

topic sentence

Then the formation changes. Green and white rays of light seems to drop straight down from above. The rays flow and form themselves into drapes that spred across the entire sky. The drapes are mostly white, but with some purple in between. A hissing noise begins as the drapes slowly disappear and then reppear in new forms.

detail sentences

After ten or fifteen minutes, the Aurora borealis starts to fade away. The formation of drapes get wider and wider, but becomes less and less distinct. The lights seem to blink on and off. Finally, they disappear altogether.

Go to page 66 in the **Practice** the Strategy **Notebook!**

Revising

Elaborate

Find appropriate pictures or create illustrations that will make my description more understandable and meaningful.

> After I finished my first draft, I read it silently to myself. My description seemed pretty clear, but I thought it might be even better if I replaced my drawings with actual aurora borealis photos. (Besides I don't really draw that well!) I found a couple of great photos on the Internet that were not copyrighted, so I downloaded them and added them to my paper. I reread my paper again to make sure the pictures I found were appropriate for what I was describing.

READ TO MYSELF

[2nd DRAFT]

I watch the sky. A great white arc of light begin to appear. It stretches larger and larger. Several more follow it. They expand. They become red and purple, especially at the edges.

Then the formation changes. Green and white rays of light seems to drop straight down from above. The rays flow and form themselves into drapes that spred across the entire sky. The drapes are mostly white, but with some purple in

between. A hissing noise begins as the drapes slowly disappear and then reppear in new forms.

Go to page 69 in the **Practice** the Strategy **Notebook!**

Descriptive Writing • Observation Report

Revising

Clarify
Make sure that I have varied sentence length and structure.

" Next, I checked my report for sentence length and structure. The **Rubric** tells me I should vary my sentences a bit. I found one paragraph that definitely needed work. I reworded and combined the sentences in it so that they sounded more interesting. "

Sentence Pattern

A sentence pattern is the order in which the parts of a sentence are arranged. Sentence patterns include subject-verb ("The dog ate.") and subject-verb-object ("The dog ate her dinner."). Using the same sentence pattern over and over again makes your writing boring. Here are some ways to get variety:

- **Begin with an adverb.**
  Gradually, the sky changes color.

- **Begin with a prepositional phrase.**
  Throughout the light show, the formations constantly change.

- **Begin with a dependent clause.**
  When the aurora borealis ends, the sky darkens again.

[3rd DRAFT]

combined sentences

prepositional phrase

As I watch ~~the sky.~~ A great white arc of light begin to appear. Across the sky It stretches larger and larger, and soon Several more follow it. ~~They expand~~ They become red and purple, especially at the edges, as they expand

combined sentences

Go to page 70 in the **Practice** the Strategy **Notebook!**

Descriptive Writing • Observation Report

Editing

Proofread

Check to see that the subject and verb in each sentence agree.

" The next thing I have to do is look for errors in my report. I always check for grammar mistakes and misspelled words. According to the **Rubric**, I should also make sure subjects agree with verbs. Agreement can sometimes be a problem for me, especially when the subject and verb are separated. It's also hard when the subject sounds plural even though it's singular—like **borealis** with its **s** on the end. "

Subject-Verb Agreement

Singular subjects take singular verbs. Plural subjects take plural verbs. Singular verbs usually end in *-s* or *-es*.

> The **aurora borealis appears** only in northern skies.

> In the lower latitudes **it occurs** rarely or never.

Compound subjects joined with *and* are nearly always plural. In compound subjects joined with *or* or *nor,* the verb agrees with the last item in the subject.

> **Chris and his mom have seen** the northern lights from their porch.

> Neither Chris's dad nor **his sisters find** the lights very interesting.

Be sure that the verb agrees with the subject and not with the object of a preposition that comes before the verb.

> An **aurora borealis** of many colors **is** an awe-inspiring sight.

> Even today, flickering **panels** of light in the sky **frighten** some people.

To make sure the subject and verb agree in a question, reword the sentence in subject-verb order.

> In which state are observers most likely to see the northern lights?
> **Observers are** mostly like to see the northern lights in which state?

Extra Practice
See **Subject-Verb Agreement** (pages CS 12–CS 13) in the back of this book.

Descriptive Writing • Observation Report

[4th DRAFT]

Observing the Aurora Borealis, or Northern Lights

Sometimes I'm really happy that we live so far north. This is the reason.

If you are lucky, on ⓈⓅ certain ~~certin~~ nights you may see the aurora borealis, or

northern lights. Here is my observation from a night last week when the

lights appeared:

It is a perfect night for a light show. The air feels crisp and cold as

a gentle breeze touches my skin. I can smell the fresh pine trees

growing in the nearby woods. Stars are ⓈⓅ twinkling ~~twinkeling~~.

As I watch, a great white arc of light — *subject-verb agreement*

begins to appear. Across the sky it stretches,

larger and larger, and soon several more

follow it. They become red and purple,

especially at the edges, as they expand.

subject-verb agreement — Then the formation changes. Green and

white rays of light seem to drop straight

down from above. The rays flow and

form themselves into drapes that ⓈⓅ spread ~~spred~~

across the entire sky. The drapes are

mostly white, but with some purple in

between. A hissing noise begins as the drapes slowly disappear and

then ⓈⓅ reappear ~~reppear~~ in new forms. — *subject-verb agreement*

After ten or fifteen minutes, the Aurora borealis starts to fade away.

The formation of drapes gets wider and wider, but becomes less and

less distinct. The lights seem to blink on and off. Finally, they disappear

altogether.

Go to page 71 in the **Practice** the Strategy ∧ **Notebook!**

Descriptive Writing • Observation Report

Publishing

Include my report in a class observation journal.

Writer:	Chris
Assignment:	observation report
Topic:	aurora borealis
Audience:	classmates and other interested readers
Method of Publication:	class observation journal
Reason for Choice:	My report was about something that doesn't occur that often and that many people have never seen. So I was sure readers would find it interesting.

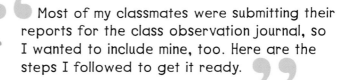

> Most of my classmates were submitting their reports for the class observation journal, so I wanted to include mine, too. Here are the steps I followed to get it ready.

1. First I checked my observation report to make sure I had corrected all errors.

2. Then I made sure my photos were securely attached to the report and positioned in the places where they belonged.

3. I put "by Chris T." at the top of the report.

4. Finally I punched holes in the side of the report so it would go easily into the binder my class was using.

Observing the Aurora Borealis, or Northern Lights

by Chris T.

Sometimes I'm really happy that we live so far north. This is the reason. If you are lucky, on certain nights you may see the aurora borealis, or northern lights. Here is my observation from a night last week when the lights appeared:

It is a perfect night for a light show. The air feels crisp and cold as a gentle breeze touches my skin. I can smell the fresh pine trees growing in the nearby woods. Stars are twinkling.

As I watch, a great white arc of light begins to appear. Across the sky it stretches, larger and larger, and soon several more follow it. They become red and purple, especially at the edges, as they expand.

Then the formation changes. Green and white rays of light seem to drop straight down from above. The rays flow and form themselves into drapes that spread across the entire sky. The drapes are mostly white, but with some purple in between. A hissing noise begins as the drapes slowly disappear and then reappear in new forms.

After ten or fifteen minutes, the aurora borealis starts to fade away. The formation of drapes gets wider and wider, but becomes less and less distinct. The lights seem to blink on and off. Finally, they disappear altogether.

USING the Rubric for Assessment

Go to pages 72–73 in the **Practice the Strategy Notebook!** Use that rubric to assess Chris's paper. Try using the rubric to assess your own writing.

your own DESCRIPTIVE writing

Social Studies

Put the strategies you practiced in this unit to work to write your own descriptive essay, observation report, or both! You can:

- develop the writing you did in the Your Own Writing pages of the *Practice the Strategy Notebook;*

- pick an idea below and write something new;

- choose another idea of your own.

Be sure to follow the steps in the writing process. Use the rubrics in this unit to assess your writing.

Descriptive Essay

- life for serfs and lords on a manor in the Middle Ages
- a city in Europe, Asia, or Africa that you would like to visit
- opening day of the 1848 Seneca Falls Convention for women's rights
- the inner workings of a television studio
- someone important in your life

Observation Report

- speakers at a televised session of the United Nations
- children who speak different languages trying to communicate with one another
- a dog and its owner going through paces at a dog show
- an athlete preparing for his or her event

portfolio

School–Home Connection

Keep a writing portfolio. Think about adding the activities from the *Practice the Strategy Notebook* to your writing portfolio. You may want to take your portfolio home to share.

PERSUASIVE writing

tries to convince the reader to accept an opinion or take an action.

1

Editorial

2

Persuasive Letter

PERSUASIVE writing

Editorial

In this chapter, you will work with one kind of persuasive writing, an **editorial**.

An **editorial** is a newspaper or magazine article expressing the editors' opinion on a specific person, place, thing, or event. A problem-solution editorial, the type you will be writing, establishes a problem and then offers a solution. It also tries to convince the reader to agree with that solution.

The article on the next page is a problem-solution editorial. Notice that the language is fairly serious and formal, and the pronoun *I* is not used.

Read the questions below. Then read the editorial, keeping the questions in mind.

 How well does the writer make the audience understand the importance of the problem?

 How clearly does the writer proceed from the problem to a possible solution and then to the desired end result?

 How well has the writer built an argument supported by facts, statistics, or other strong examples?

 How consistently does the writer avoid including unsound or irrelevant facts or examples?

 How well does the writer use and punctuate appositives (phrases describing nouns)?

Turn It Off!

by The Editors of
the *Springfield Middle School Gazette*

When was the last time you read a good book, a modern novel or a classic, in the evening? How long ago was it that you went camping or just took a weekend hike in the woods? There was a time when people were likely to get involved in pastimes like these. Now, though, the most common activity in many people's lives is watching television. Sad to say, this is not much of an "activity" at all. According to recent research compiled by RealVision, a program that gives facts about television, the average teenager watches television more than 20 hours per week. By the age of eighteen, that teenager will have seen more than 200,000 violent acts and more than 16,000 murders. He or she may be bombarded with as many as 20,000 commercials in a year. At the same time, due to lack of any real activity, that teenager's likelihood of becoming seriously overweight rises steadily. Clearly, something is wrong here!

As a school, we can take steps to do something about excessive television watching and the problems it causes. Our suggestion is that we participate in the national TV-Turnoff Week next April. More than 3,000 groups, many of them schools, were part of this event last year. Most students who were involved thought it was just great! They found that they had time to do many more things. Some listened to music. Others read or exercised. Still others cooked, made scrapbooks, and played board games. Some even began talking to their brothers and sisters again! For a small fee the TV-Turnoff Network, a not-for-profit organization that encourages less television watching, can provide our school with planning booklets to get us started. It can also supply posters and T-shirts to keep us motivated. Teachers can hold classroom discussions about activities to replace television. Once enough students become interested, it shouldn't be hard to get the whole school to participate.

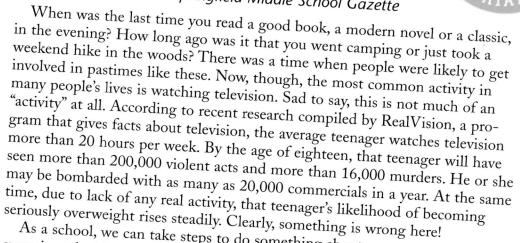

Will one week away from staring at screens change our lives? It's hard to know. Many students who joined TV-Turnoff Week in the past said it really made a difference for them. It provided a springboard for breaking old viewing habits. With luck, the program can do the same for us.

Using a Rubric

A rubric is a tool that tells "what counts" in a piece of writing.

How do you use a rubric? You assign 1, 2, 3, or 4 points to qualities in the writing. These points show how well the author dealt with the various qualities.

The questions on page 148 were used to make this rubric.

"Hi! I'm Doria. I'm learning about problem-solution editorials, too. What did you think of the editorial on page 149? Read this rubric. Begin with the questions; then go on to read the scoring information for each question. We'll be using the rubric to evaluate the editorial you just read."

Audience
How well does the writer make the audience understand the importance of the problem?

Organization
How clearly does the writer proceed from the problem to a possible solution and then to the desired end result?

Elaboration
How well has the writer built an argument supported by facts, statistics, or other strong examples?

Clarification
How consistently does the writer avoid including unsound or irrelevant facts or examples?

Conventions & Skills
How well does the writer use and punctuate appositives (phrases that describe nouns)?

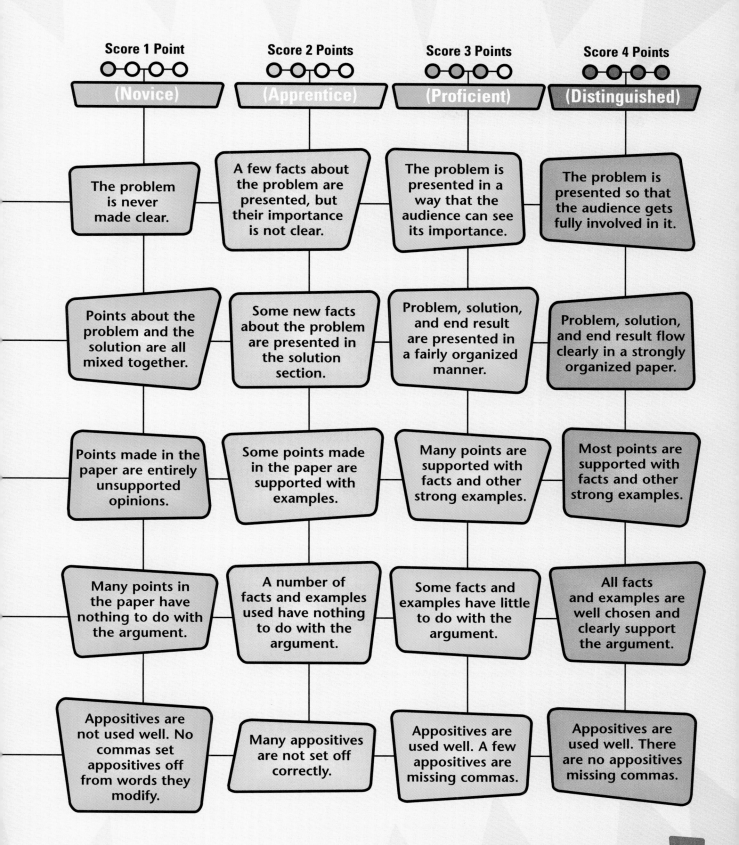

Score 1 Point
(Novice)

Score 2 Points
(Apprentice)

Score 3 Points
(Proficient)

Score 4 Points
(Distinguished)

The problem is never made clear.

A few facts about the problem are presented, but their importance is not clear.

The problem is presented in a way that the audience can see its importance.

The problem is presented so that the audience gets fully involved in it.

Points about the problem and the solution are all mixed together.

Some new facts about the problem are presented in the solution section.

Problem, solution, and end result are presented in a fairly organized manner.

Problem, solution, and end result flow clearly in a strongly organized paper.

Points made in the paper are entirely unsupported opinions.

Some points made in the paper are supported with examples.

Many points are supported with facts and other strong examples.

Most points are supported with facts and other strong examples.

Many points in the paper have nothing to do with the argument.

A number of facts and examples used have nothing to do with the argument.

Some facts and examples have little to do with the argument.

All facts and examples are well chosen and clearly support the argument.

Appositives are not used well. No commas set appositives off from words they modify.

Many appositives are not set off correctly.

Appositives are used well. A few appositives are missing commas.

Appositives are used well. There are no appositives missing commas.

Using a Rubric to Study the Model

With your classmates, discuss each question on the rubric. Find sentences and paragraphs in the model that help you answer each question. Then use the rubric to assess the editorial on each question.

How well does the writer make the audience understand the importance of the problem?

> The audience for this editorial is students about our age. I notice that all the examples the author presents have to do with teenagers. Showing that the problem had to do with **me** was a great way to get my attention!

. . . the average teenager watches television more than 20 hours per week. By the age of eighteen, that teenager will have seen more than 200,000 violent acts and more than 16,000 murders. He or she may be bombarded with as many as 20,000 commercials in a year. At the same time, due to lack of any real activity, that teenager's likelihood of becoming seriously overweight rises steadily.

How clearly does the writer proceed from the problem to a possible solution and then to the desired end result?

" The editorial has three paragraphs, and each paragraph has its own purpose. Paragraph 1 presents the problem. Paragraph 2 offers a solution. Paragraph 3 tells what the end result could be. Look at the words in each paragraph that the writer uses to do this. "

Problem (paragraph 1):

. . . the most common activity in many people's lives is watching television. Sad to say, this is not much of an "activity" at all.

Solution (paragraph 2):

Our suggestion is that we participate in the national TV-Turnoff Week next April.

End Result (paragraph 3):

Many students who joined TV-Turnoff Week in the past said it really made a difference for them.

How well has the writer built an argument supported by facts, statistics, or other strong examples?

" Remember how well the writer used all those facts and figures in connecting the problem to teenagers? The writer also built a strong case in recommending a solution, by giving specific examples from the last TV-Turnoff Week. "

More than 3,000 groups, many of them schools, were part of this event last year. Most students who were involved thought it was just great! They found that they had time to do many more things. Some listened to music. Others read or exercised. Still others cooked, made scrapbooks, and played board games. Some even began talking to their brothers and sisters again!

Clarification

How consistently does the writer avoid including unsound or irrelevant facts or examples?

" I can see that all the information the writer used in both the problem and the solution sections is useful and important. For example, the writer knew that the audience would want to know about how to organize the TV-Turnoff Week. So the editorial includes information about the national organizers and the help they could give. "

For a small fee the TV-Turnoff Network, a not-for-profit organization that encourages less television watching, can provide our school with planning booklets to get us started. It can also supply posters and T-shirts to keep us motivated.

Conventions & Skills

How well does the writer use and punctuate appositives (phrases describing nouns)?

" All the words in the editorial are spelled and capitalized correctly. I noticed that the writer remembered to put commas both before and after appositives. Here is an example. "

When was the last time you read a good book, **a modern novel or a classic,** in the evening?

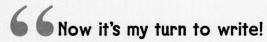

Now it's my turn to write!

I'm going to write a problem-solution editorial of my own. Follow along and notice how I use the model and the rubric to help me practice good writing strategies. "

DoRia

Writer of an Editorial

Name: Doria

Home: Indiana

Hobbies and Interests: antique cars, going ice skating in the winter

Favorite Book: *Link Across America: A Story of the Historic Lincoln Highway* by Mary Elizabeth Anderson

Favorite Food: corn on the cob

Assignment: problem-solution editorial

Prewriting

Gather
Brainstorm to choose a problem for which I can propose a solution.

❝I know I'm always seeing problems around school that bother me, but then I get distracted and forget about them. Brainstorming with some kids from my class—everybody volunteering suggestions about problems that they've noticed—was a strategy that really helped me focus on a topic. Here are some ideas we put on the board.❞

- cafeteria: always dirty
- library: needs to be open before school
- too much bullying in the hallways
- activity period: should be longer

"I chose a problem that I not only knew about, but had some definite ideas about how we could solve: bullying. I kept brainstorming by myself for more ideas and then wrote them down. ❞

The Problem: Bullying

- happens in hallways, washrooms
- could happen to anyone
- cause of violence in some schools (get examples)
- everyone afraid to rat on others
- some kids get hurt
- smaller kids are scared

We need:
- "no tolerance" policy
- help from teachers
- tables-turned activities —(see what it's like)
- more student involvement
- schoolwide campaign

Go to page 74 in the **Practice** the Strategy **Notebook!**

Prewriting

Organize   Make a problem-solution frame.

66 I know from the **Rubric** that it's important to organize my information. My strategy was to organize my details into a problem-solution frame. I tried to include details that would really hit home with my audience, the kids in my school. 99

Problem-Solution Frame

A **problem-solution frame** defines the problem and organizes information to solve the problem.

Problem Box

What is the problem?
• bullying

Why is it a problem?
• smaller kids scared
• some kids get hurt
• cause of violence in some schools (need examples)
• everyone afraid to rat on other students

Who has the problem?
• our school does, in the hallways and washrooms

Solution Box

Solutions
• schoolwide campaign
• "no tolerance" policy
• help from teachers
• tables-turned activities
• more student involvement

Results
• make everyone conscious of the problem
• everyone knows rules and what will happen if they're broken
• keep things from happening by supervising washrooms, little-used hallways
• show bullies what it feels like
• can show disapproval, can recommend ways to change things

End Result Box
may not totally solve problem, but will be a great start toward stopping bullies

Go to page 76 in the **Practice** the Strategy **Notebook!**

Drafting

" To make my editorial really strong, my strategy is to present my ideas in a clear, organized way. I also want my audience to understand the importance of the problem. In my introduction, I'll make sure that I focus on things that are happening in our school—and what could happen if we ignore the problem. Then I'll follow my problem-solution frame to develop my body and conclusion.

"When I draft, I'll concentrate on getting my ideas down. If I find that I need a few details from outside sources to strengthen my argument, I can get them later. "

Introduction, Body, Conclusion

The **introduction** is the first paragraph of a paper. A good introduction grabs the audience's attention and states the main idea of the paper.

In a problem-solution editorial, use the introductory paragraph to explain the **problem**.

The **body** is the main part of your writing. The body comes between the introduction and conclusion and develops your main ideas.

In a problem-solution editorial, use one or more body paragraphs to present ideas for a **solution**.

The **conclusion** is the last paragraph of a longer paper. The conclusion ties up loose ends and summarizes main points.

In a problem-solution editorial, use the conclusion to **explain the results the solution may provide**.

Stop the Bullying

introduction

Yesterday a ~~little~~ sixth grader was found hiding near the janitor's closet. Someone finally got him to admit, "~~Sam~~ XXX ~~an eighth grader~~ is after me." (XXX, an eighth grader has a reputation for bullying smaller students.) Last week, another sixth grader went to class with his shirt ripped and a scrach on his face. Though he wouldn't say what happened, a lot of kids knew that he had had a run-in with YYY, another bully. Allmost any student in our School could give more examples like these. Bullying, a bigger or stronger kid terrorizing a smaller or weaker one is happening all the time in our hallways and washrooms. It's happened in alot of other schools, and its caused alot of difficulties.

problem

solution

The best solution for this problem is a schoolwide campaign against bullying. Everyone can play ~~their~~ a part. First, the administration should make it clear that they know bullying is going on, and that they don't approve of it. Students and teachers, the people most likely to witness bullying must play an active part. Students must learn to show that they don't approve of bullying behaveior. Students must become convinced that there is nothing wrong with reporting bullying behaveior to someone in authority. But they must also have a way of keeping their names confidenshul. Teachers can patrol hallways and washrooms the places where bullying goes on most. And they should make it clear that bullies will be punished. In fact, teachers can give bullies a taste of their own medecine by having kids in their classes gang up on the bullies!

body

Bullying has been going on around here for a long time, so we probably won't get rid of it over night. But if we start some new policies, and make sure everyone follows up on them, we can make a real start on solving the problem.

conclusion

result

Go to page 78 in the **Practice** the Strategy **Notebook!**

Revising

Elaborate

Make sure I have facts, statistics, examples, and/or anecdotes to explain the problem.

66 I wanted to see if my first draft made sense, so I read it to my partner, Ferris. He liked that I followed the **Rubric** and used real-life anecdotes from our school. But he thought I should say more about problems bullying has caused in other schools. I found some good examples and statistics on the Internet and added them to my editorial. 99

READ TO A PARTNER

Statistics

Statistics are facts presented in numerical form, such as ratios, percentages, and summaries.

Anecdotes

An **anecdote** is a very brief story used to make a point. It is often used in the same way an example would be used.

[2nd DRAFT]

. . . terrorizing a smaller or weaker one is happening all the time in our hallways and washrooms. ~~It's happened in alot of other schools, and its~~ ~~caused alot of difficulties.~~ And this is not a problem we can ignore. When the World Health Organization sponsored a recent survey of more than
statistic
↳ 15,000 students, it found that more than 10 percent of the students were bullied "sometimes" or "weekly." Some parents have removed their children from school because the bullying got so bad. ← fact

---

Go to page 79 in the **Practice** the Strategy **Notebook!**

Revising

Clarify

Check my rationale. Get rid of any points that are unsound or do not support my solution.

"Ferris thought that my idea of ganging up on bullies was really a bad one. If I wanted to convince my audience that my No Tolerance solution was good, I couldn't suggest fighting meanness with more meanness. Once I saw that that rationale would probably turn off my audience, I dropped the idea from my paper and came up with one that my audience would think was more reasonable."

Rationale

A **rationale** is the underlying principle behind a line of thought or opinion. For example, a rationale behind the opinion "I want a dog" might be that "Dogs are good pets who protect the home."

[3rd DRAFT]

. . . witness bullying must play an active part. Students must learn to show that they don't approve of bullying behaveior. Students must become convinced that there is nothing wrong with reporting bullying behaveior to someone in authority. But they must also have a way of keeping their names confidenshul. Teachers can patrol hallways and washrooms the places where bullying goes on most. And they should make it clear that bullies will be punished. ~~In fact, teachers can give bullies a taste of their own medecine by having kids in their classes gang up on the bullies.~~ They can also use homeroom periods to give individual guideance.

unsound solution

better solution

Go to page 80 in the **Practice the Strategy Notebook!**

Editing

Proofread
Check to see that appositives are used well and set off by commas.

> Now I need to look for errors. I know I have a few spelling mistakes. But the **Rubric** also tells me to make sure I've used and punctuated appositives correctly. It's easy to forget the comma at the end of an appositive.

Conventions & SKILLS

Appositives

An **appositive** is a phrase that identifies a noun. It follows the noun and is usually set off from the rest of the sentence with commas.

Some schools institute a No Tolerance policy, **a way of making sure that all bullying is punished.**

Teachers and students, **the most likely people to witness bullying,** must be on the alert for it.

Notice that when an appositive is in the middle of a sentence, a comma comes both before and after it.

Extra Practice
See **Appositives** (pages CS 14–CS 15) in the back of this book.

Persuasive Writing • Editorial

Proofreading Marks

⌐ Indent.
≡ Make a capital.
/ Make a small letter.
∧ Add something.
ℓ Take out something.
⊙ Add a period.
New paragraph
SP Spelling error

[4th DRAFT]

Stop the Bullying

Yesterday a sixth grader was found hiding near the janitor's closet. Someone finally got him to admit, "XXX is after me." (XXX, an eighth grader has a reputation for bullying smaller students.) Last week, another sixth grader went to class with his shirt ripped and a ~~scrach~~ **scratch** on his face. Though he wouldn't say what happened, a lot of kids knew that he had had a run-in with YYY, another bully. ~~Allmost~~ **Almost** any student in our School could give more examples like these. Bullying, a bigger or stronger kid terrorizing a smaller or weaker one, is happening all the time in our hallways and washrooms. And this is not a problem we can ignore. When the World Health Organization sponsored a recent survey of more than 15,000 students, it found that more than 10 percent of the students were bullied "sometimes" or "weekly." Some parents have removed their children from school because the bullying got so bad.

appositive

The best solution for this problem is a schoolwide campaign against bullying. Everyone can play a part. First, the administration should make it clear that they know bullying is going on, and that they don't approve of it. Then, they should announce that they are adopting a "No ~~Tolerence~~ **Tolerance**" policy for bullies. This means that every time someone is caught ~~bulling~~ **bullying** another student, the bully will be punished. Students and teachers, the people most likely to witness bullying, must play an active part. Students must learn to show that they don't approve of bullying ~~behaveior.~~ **behavior** ~~Students~~ They must become convinced that there is nothing wrong with reporting bullying ~~behaveior~~ **behavior** to someone in authority.

appositive

Go to page 81 in the **Practice the Strategy Notebook!**

Persuasive Writing · Editorial   163

Publishing

Share Publish my editorial in the school newspaper.

Writer:	Doria
Assignment:	editorial
Topic:	bullying and how to stop it
Audience:	students, teachers, administrators
Method of Publication:	school newspaper
Reason for Choice:	I wanted to reach as big an audience as I could.

> " Our school paper asked for volunteers to write editorials about school problems. I submitted my editorial, and the paper accepted it! Here's what I did to get it ready. "

1. First, I read my editorial again to make sure my thinking was sound and my writing was clear.

2. Then I checked my paper once more for any errors in spelling, punctuation, and grammar.

3. I typed it up neatly.

4. I remembered NOT to put "by Doria G." after my title, because editorials aren't signed by the writer.

Stop the Bullying

Yesterday a sixth grader was found hiding near the janitor's closet. Someone finally got him to admit, "XXX is after me." (XXX, an eighth grader, has a reputation for bullying smaller students.) Last week, another sixth grader went to class with his shirt ripped and a scratch on his face. Though he wouldn't say what happened, a lot of kids knew that he had had a run-in with YYY, another bully. Almost any student in our school could give more examples like these. Bullying, a bigger or stronger kid terrorizing a smaller or weaker one, is happening all the time in our hallways and washrooms. And this is not a problem we can ignore. When the World Health Organization sponsored a recent survey of more than 15,000 students, it found that more than 10 percent of the students were bullied "sometimes" or "weekly." Some parents have removed their children from school because the bullying got so bad.

The best solution for this problem is a schoolwide campaign against bullying. Everyone can play a part. First, the administration should make it clear that they know bullying is going on, and that they don't approve of it. Then, they should announce that they are adopting a "No Tolerance" policy for bullies. This means that every time someone is caught bullying another student, the bully will be punished. Students and teachers, the people most likely to witness bullying, must play an active part. Students must learn to show that they don't approve of bullying behavior. They must become convinced that there is nothing wrong with reporting bullying behavior to someone in authority. But they must also have a way of keeping their names confidential. Teachers can patrol hallways and washrooms, the places where bullying goes on most. And they should make it clear that bullies will be punished. They can also use homeroom periods to give individual guidance.

Bullying has been going on around here for a long time, so we probably won't get rid of it overnight. But if we start some new policies, and make sure everyone follows up on them, we can make a real start on solving the problem.

USING the Rubric for Assessment

Go to pages 82–83 in the **Practice** the Strategy **Notebook!** Use that rubric to assess Doria's paper. Try using the rubric to assess your own writing.

PERSUASIVE writing

Persuasive Letter

This chapter will give you a chance to do one kind of persuasive writing, a **persuasive letter**.

A **persuasive letter** gives the writer's opinion about a subject and tries to convince the audience—the person or organization to whom the letter is addressed—that the opinion is valid or worthy of consideration.

On the next page you will find a persuasive business letter. First, read the questions below. Then read the letter, keeping the questions in mind as you read.

 **Audience** How quickly and clearly is the writer's opinion presented to the reader?

 **Organization** How consistently does the writer use paragraphs with strong, clear topic sentences to present reasons for the opinion?

 **Elaboration** How effectively do detail sentences support topic sentences in paragraphs?

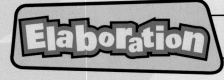 **Clarification** How clear and correct is the writer's use of homophones and other confusing words?

 **Conventions & Skills** How carefully does the writer follow correct business-letter form? How well does the writer avoid double negatives?

heading → 38 Oak Lane
Ridge Park, IL 60100
November 12, 20--

Director of Children's Services
Municipal Services of Ridge Park
455 Laurel Road
Ridge Park, IL 60100 ← inside address

Dear Sir or Madam: ← salutation

A group of families from Nigeria has recently moved into our area. About 20 students from these families are enrolled at my school, Trout Junior High. These students need special services to help them adapt to living here, help that your agency could provide. The following are some of the reasons I think you should assist them.

To begin with, these students are in dire need of translators or other language helpers. Our school has special classes for non-English speakers. However, the teachers know little about these students' language. If translators could work with students in their regular classes, I know it would help them. Right now, they just sit quietly and shake their heads when a teacher calls on them. After two months of school, they still can barely communicate with us.

Another thing the students need help with is proper clothing for the winter. You might help them just by providing some warm hand-me-downs. However, I think it would be even better if you could get them some new, in-style clothing. That way, they could start to feel like they fit in with the other students.

A final reason to help the students is this: to become real Americans, they need help understanding our culture. For example, we have many holidays coming up in the next few months. Someone needs to help the new students understand the history, meaning, and customs of these holidays. It would also be good to introduce them to things like American foods and sports. Culture classes, where students could ask questions in their own language without feeling embarrassed, would be one way to handle this.

As you can see, there are many ways you could help our new students. Please consider taking on some or all of these projects.

closing → Yours truly,

signature ↙

Susan Bernini

Susan Bernini

Using a Rubric

You already know that a rubric is a tool that tells "what counts" in a piece of writing.

How do you use a rubric? You assign 1, 2, 3, or 4 points to qualities in the writing. These points show how well the author dealt with the various qualities.

The questions on page 166 were used to make this rubric.

"Hi! Let me introduce myself. I'm Leon, and I'm learning about persuasive letters, too. What did you think of the letter on page 167? Have a look at this rubric. Start with the questions; then read the information for each question. We'll use the rubric to evaluate the letter you just read."

Audience
How quickly and clearly is the writer's opinion presented to the reader?

Organization
How consistently does the writer use paragraphs with strong, clear topic sentences to present reasons for the opinion?

Elaboration
How effectively do detail sentences support topic sentences in paragraphs?

Clarification
How clear and correct is the writer's use of homophones and other confusing words?

Conventions & Skills
How carefully does the writer follow correct business-letter form? How well does the writer avoid double negatives?

Score 1 Point	Score 2 Points	Score 3 Points	Score 4 Points
(Novice)	**(Apprentice)**	**(Proficient)**	**(Distinguished)**
The writer's opinion is never made clear to the reader.	The writer's opinion is not made clear to the reader until the end of the letter.	The writer's opinion is given in a somewhat long introductory paragraph.	The writer's opinion is given in a brief, clear introductory paragraph.
Paragraphs generally do not have topic sentences.	Paragraphs have topic sentences, but they don't always give reasons for the writer's opinion.	Paragraphs have topic sentences, and most give reasons for the writer's opinion.	Paragraphs consistently have topic sentences that give reasons for the writer's opinion.
Details are mostly unrelated to topic sentences.	Details sometimes support topic sentences.	Most details support topic sentences, but a few are unrelated.	All details provide strong support for topic sentences.
The writer uses the wrong word many times.	The writer has several errors with homophones and other confusing words.	The writer occasionally uses the wrong word.	The writer always uses the correct homophone or other easily confused word.
The letter is missing several parts, and there are many double negatives.	The letter is missing at least one part, and there are several double negatives.	The letter has all basic parts, but there are a few errors in them and with double negatives.	The letter has all basic parts, and there are no errors with them or with double negatives.

Using a Rubric
to Study the Model

Discuss each question on the rubric with your classmates. Then use the rubric to evaluate Susan Bernini's persuasive letter on each question. Find sentences and paragraphs in the letter that help you answer each question.

 **Audience** — How quickly and clearly is the writer's opinion presented to the reader?

" The whole purpose of the letter's first paragraph is to introduce the writer's opinion to the audience in a clear, easy-to-understand way. The writer gives a little bit of background—but just enough to show what the issue is. "

A group of families from Nigeria has recently moved into our area. About 20 students from these families are enrolled at my school, Trout Junior High. These students need special services to help them adapt to living here, help that your agency could provide. The following are some of the reasons I think you should assist them.

How consistently does the writer use paragraphs with strong, clear topic sentences to present reasons for the opinion?

"The writer has three main reasons for her opinion, and she makes each one the topic sentence of a paragraph. Just by looking at those topic sentences, I got a good sense of what her argument was."

Reason/Topic Sentence 1: To begin with, these students are in dire need of translators or other language helpers.
Reason/Topic Sentence 2: Another thing the students need help with is proper clothing for the winter.
Reason/Topic Sentence 3: A final reason to help the students is this: to become real Americans, they need help understanding our culture.

How effectively do detail sentences support topic sentences in paragraphs?

"All the details in the writer's paragraphs give either facts or examples to support the topic sentences. Notice how that works in this paragraph."

Another thing the students need help with is proper clothing for the winter. You might help them just by providing some warm hand-me-downs. However, I think it would be even better if you could get them some new, in-style clothing. That way, they could start to feel like they fit in with the other students.

Clarification

How clear and correct is the writer's use of homophones and other confusing words?

" The writer hasn't made any mistakes with homophones or other easily confused words, as far as I can see. For example, the writer uses **your**—not **you're**—when describing the reader's agency. Look at these sentences. Notice how each underlined word is used correctly. "

These students <u>need</u> special services <u>to</u> help them <u>adapt</u> to living <u>here</u>, help that <u>your</u> agency could provide.

<u>Right</u> now, they just <u>sit</u> quietly and shake <u>their</u> heads when a teacher calls on them.

Conventions & Skills

How carefully does the writer follow correct business-letter form? How well does the writer avoid double negatives?

" All the parts of a business letter are included, with correct capitalization and punctuation. And the writer avoids double negatives, including those with **barely** or **hardly,** as in this sentence. "

After two months of school, they still can barely communicate with us.

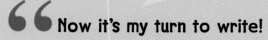

" Now it's my turn to write!

I'm going to write my own persuasive letter. Watch me as I work. I'm going to use the model and also the rubric to help me practice good writing strategies. "

LEON

Writer of a Persuasive Letter

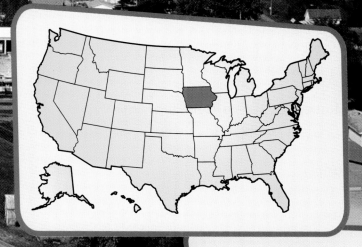

Name:	Leon
Home:	Iowa
Hobbies:	reading, bicycling, tutoring younger children
Favorite Book:	*Tour de France/Tour de Force: A Visual History of the World's Greatest Bicycle Race* by James Startt
Favorite Teacher:	Mrs. Garza, my social studies teacher
Assignment:	persuasive letter

PrewRiting

Gather

Choose an issue that I have a strong opinion about, and a person who could change things. List reasons, facts, and examples to support my opinion.

"I knew the school board was planning to stop buying new books for our school library. I wanted to present my opinion against this idea, so I had no trouble coming up with a topic for my persuasive letter. I decided the best person to send my letter to was the school board president, Ms. Williams.

"My strategy was to list reasons, facts, and examples that would support my idea. My reasons would explain my idea, and facts and examples I included would explain and support my reasons. I knew that all three were important if I wanted to convince Ms. Williams to continue buying new books.

"I did a lot of thinking, and even a little research, to get more details."

Opinion:

Don't stop buying new books.

Reasons:

- need accurate, up-to-date information
- need recent books students can understand

Facts/Examples:

- lots of research projects
- info about human genome project: library books really out of date
- Internet articles sometimes too difficult to help (written for scientists)
- lots of current nonfiction books written for students our age

Go to page 84 in the **Practice the Strategy Notebook!**

Persuasive Writing • Persuasive Letter

Prewriting

Organize
Make a persuasion map to organize reasons, facts, and examples to support my call to action.

" My next step was to organize my lists in a persuasion map.

"Making my persuasion map was easy because I had already separated facts and examples from reasons in my earlier notes. On the map, I listed my reasons first. Then I filled in the facts and examples where they made the most sense. After looking over the map, I wasn't sure I had enough examples to support each reason. I thought I would probably have to add to my map, so I started thinking about other examples I might use. I also came up with a call to action. "

Persuasion Map

A **persuasion map** organizes reasons, supporting examples, and facts that show that the reasons make sense. All this leads to a call to action, a direct invitation to the audience to do something.

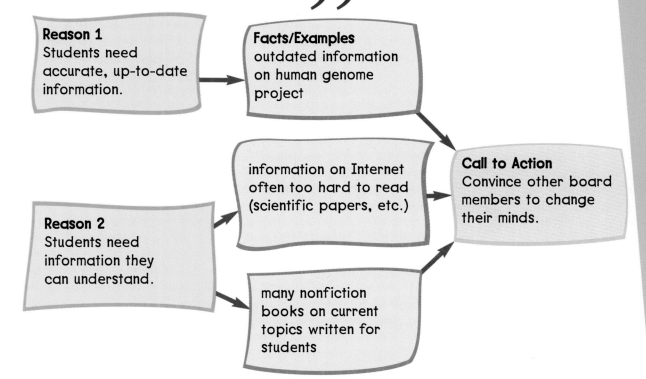

Reason 1
Students need accurate, up-to-date information.

Facts/Examples
outdated information on human genome project

information on Internet often too hard to read (scientific papers, etc.)

Reason 2
Students need information they can understand.

many nonfiction books on current topics written for students

Call to Action
Convince other board members to change their minds.

Go to page 86 in the **Practice** the Strategy **Notebook!**

Drafting

Write
Draft the body of my letter. Use topic sentences to present the reasons for my opinion.

> Because of all the planning and research I'd done, it was pretty easy to draft my letter. I knew I should state my opinion in my first paragraph. After that, I followed the strategy of presenting each of my reasons as the topic sentences in my next two paragraphs. I put my call to action in my final paragraph.
>
> "As I drafted, I concentrated on getting my ideas down. I knew I could check for spelling, capitalization, and grammar errors later.

Topic Sentence

The **topic sentence** states the main idea of a paragraph. While it is often the first sentence in the paragraph, it may also be positioned in the middle or at the end of the paragraph.

In a persuasive letter, presenting your reasons as topic sentences at the beginning of each paragraph makes your argument easy for the audience to follow and understand.

Dear Ms. Williams,

I heard on the local news that the school board was having budget problems. One solution that the board perposed was to stop buying new books for our school libraries. I am a student at Thompson Middle School, and I think that not buying library books would be a big mistake. Here are my reasons for my opinion.

topic sentence → *opinion*

Students need accurite, up-to-date information on scientific and political events. For example, I was recently asked to do a class report on the human genome project. The book in our school library said that all human genes would be identified "in the next ten years." My mother told me, though, that the identification was actually completed. None of our library books weren't current enough to have this information. Students can't hardly do accurate research in books like these.

Another reason to continue buying library books is that we students need information we can understand. You might think that we can get all the information we need on the Internet. The Internet, tho, isn't hardly always to helpful. I tried to find information on the human genome project their. All I could find were papers written by scientists for other scientists. We need more then that. We need nonfiction books by people who right just for students if we're going to do a good job on our research.

topic sentence

I hope my letter has convinced you how important it is to buy new library books. Please try to convince the other school board members to change their minds on this issue.

call to action

Go to page 89 in the **Practice** the Strategy **Notebook!**

Revising

Elaborate

Make sure detail sentences in my paragraphs provide strong support for the topic sentence.

> After I finished my first draft, I read it silently to myself. I followed the **Rubric** and checked that my detail sentences gave good support to my topic sentences. In my paragraph about needing current information, I thought I needed another example. I needed to strengthen the case I was trying to present to Ms. Williams.

Detail Sentence

A **detail sentence** supports the paragraph's main idea. The detail sentences in one paragraph should go with or tell about the main idea.

[2nd DRAFT]

topic sentence

detail sentences

Students need accurite, up-to-date information on scientific and political events. For example, I was recently asked to do a class report on the human genome project. The book in our school library said that all human genes would be identified "in the next ten years." My mother told me, though, that the identification was actually completed. None of our library books weren't current enough to have this information. Students can't hardly do accurate research in books like these.

Hear is another, even worse example. The world atlas in our library shows Germany divided into two separate countries, though it was reunited in 1990!

added detail sentence

Go to page 91 in the **Practice** the Strategy **Notebook!**

Revising

Clarify
Check to make sure that I have not misused homophones or other easily confused words.

" The Rubric tells me to check my use of words. I know that homophones and pairs of words that sound similar and have similar meanings can be tricky. I found a paragraph where I had made several careless errors by using the wrong word. I went back and made some changes. "

Easily Confused Words

Easily confused words include homophones and words with similar sounds and meanings. A **homophone** is a word that sounds the same as another word but has a different meaning and spelling. For example, *they're*, *their*, and *there* are homophones.

Other easily confused words include *sit* and *set* and *lie* and *lay*. These words have similar meanings or sounds and may be easily confused.

[3rd DRAFT]

Another reason to continue buying library books is that we students

need information we can understand. You might think that we can get all

the information we need on the Internet. The Internet, tho, isn't hardly

homophones → too
always ~~to~~ helpful. I tried to find information on the human genome

there
project ~~their.~~ All I could find were papers written by scientists for other

than
scientists. We need more ~~then~~ that. We need nonfiction books by people

write
who ~~right~~ just for students if we're going to do a good job on our

research.

homophones

easily confused word

Go to page 92 in the **Practice** the Strategy **Notebook!**

Editing

Proofread

Make sure business-letter form is correct and that there are no double negatives.

> "I thought the body of my letter was OK, but I needed to add a heading, inside address, salutation, and closing. According to the **Rubric**, I also needed to make sure I hadn't used any double negatives."

Business-Letter Form

The **heading** of a letter gives the writer's full address and the date. Commas separate city and state, and date and year. Each word is capitalized.

> 1106 Fifth Avenue
> New York, NY 10028
> September 24, 20--

The **inside address** gives the recipient's name, title (if the person has one), and full address. If the receiver's name is not known, the title can be used alone. Each important word is capitalized.

> Personnel Director
> Appleby and Company
> 25 S. Lake Road
> Oshkosh, WI 54903

The **salutation** includes the receiver's title and last name, followed by a colon. All appropriate words are capitalized.

> Dear Dr. Lopez:
> Dear Madam President:

The **closing** begins with a capital letter and is followed by a comma. The **signature** comes after the closing.

> Sincerely yours,
> *Susan Bernini*

Double Negatives

Negative words are words like *no, not, nothing, nobody, never, nowhere, neither, none,* and the contraction *n't*. Do not use more than one negative word to express a negative idea.

> The school board does**n't** have **any** money for more books. [**Not:** The school board doesn't have no money. . . .]

Hardly, barely, scarcely, and *without* are also considered to be negative words and should not be paired with another negative.

> You **can scarcely** find any recent books in our library. [**Not:** You can't scarcely. . . .]

Extra Practice

See **Business-Letter Form, Double Negatives** (pages CS 16–CS 17) in the back of this book.

[4th DRAFT]

correct business-letter form

R. R. 4, box 6

Waverton, IA 50600

April 23, 20--

Ms. Corrine Williams

School board President

Consolidated district 2

456 Travis Road

Waverton, IA 50600

correct business-letter form

correct business-letter form

Dear Ms. Williams,:

I heard on the local news that the school board was having budget problems. One solution that the board perposed (SP) *proposed* was to stop buying new books for our school libraries. I am a student at Thompson Middle School, and I think that not buying library books would be a big mistake. Here are my reasons for my opinion.

Students need accurite (SP) *accurate*, up-to-date information on scientific and political events. For example, I was recently asked to do a class report on the human genome project. The book in our school library said that all human genes would be identified "in the next ten years." My mother told me, though, that the identification was actually completed. None of our library books weren't current enough to have this information. **double negative**

Hear (SP) *Here* is another, even worse example. The world atlas in our library shows Germany divided into two separate countries, though it was reunited in 1990! Students can't hardly do accurate research in books like these. **double negative**

Go to page 93 in the **Practice** the Strategy **Notebook!**

Publishing

Share   Mail my letter to the appropriate person.

Writer:	Leon
Assignment:	persuasive letter
Topic:	buying books for the school library
Audience:	Ms. Williams, head of the school board
Method of Publication:	send by U.S. mail
Reason for Choice:	I thought I had good reasons that the school board should continue buying library books for our school, so I wanted to share my reasons with someone who could make a difference.

" I was really anxious to send my letter to Ms. Williams. Maybe I'd even get a letter back! Here is what I did to get my letter ready. "

1. First, I checked my letter to make sure I had corrected all errors.

2. Then I typed it neatly and printed it on good paper.

3. I signed my full name just above my typed name at the end.

4. Next, I addressed the envelope, using the inside address in the letter.

5. I put my return address and a stamp on the envelope, inserted the letter, and sealed and mailed it.

R. R. 4, Box 6
Waverton, IA 50600
April 23, 20--

Ms. Corrine Williams
School Board President
Consolidated District 2
456 Travis Road
Waverton, IA 50600

Dear Ms. Williams:

I heard on the local news that the school board was having budget problems. One solution that the board proposed was to stop buying new books for our school libraries. I am a student at Thompson Middle School, and I think that not buying library books would be a big mistake. Here are my reasons for my opinion.

Students need accurate, up-to-date information on recent scientific and political events. For example, I was recently asked to do a class report on the Human Genome Project. The book in our school library said that all human genes would be identified "in the next ten years." My mother told me, though, that the identification was actually completed. None of our library books were current enough to have this information. Here is another, even worse example. The world atlas in our library shows Germany divided into two separate countries, though it was reunited in 1990! Students can hardly do accurate research in books like these.

Another reason to continue buying library books is that we students need information we can understand. You might think that we can get all the information we need on the Internet. The Internet, though, isn't always too helpful. I tried to find information on the human genome there. All I could find were papers written by scientists for other scientists. We need more than that. We need nonfiction books by people who write just for students if we're going to do a good job on our research.

I hope my letter has convinced you how important it is to buy new library books. Please try to convince the other school board members to change their minds on this issue.

Yours truly,

Leon Tenant

Leon Tenant

Persuasive Writing • Persuasive Letter

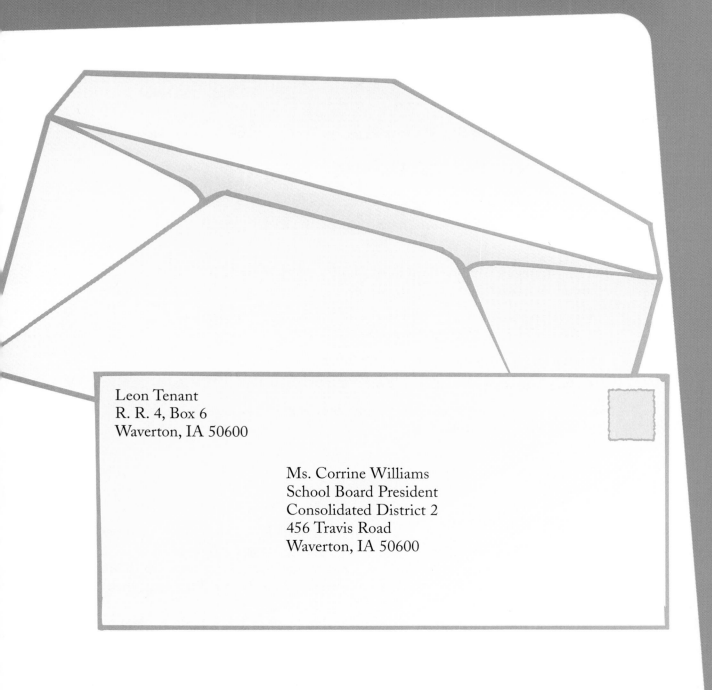

Leon Tenant
R. R. 4, Box 6
Waverton, IA 50600

Ms. Corrine Williams
School Board President
Consolidated District 2
456 Travis Road
Waverton, IA 50600

USING the Rubric for Assessment

Go to pages 94–95 in the Practice the Strategy Notebook! Use that rubric to assess Leon's letter. Try using the rubric to assess your own writing.

your own PERSUASIVE writing

Science

Put the strategies you practiced in this unit to work to write your own editorial, persuasive letter, or both! You can:

- develop the writing you did in the Your Own Writing pages of the *Practice the Strategy Notebook;*
- pick an idea below and write something new;
- choose another idea of your own.

Be sure to follow the steps in the writing process. Use the rubrics in this unit to assess your writing.

Editorial

- saving on high heating costs by developing an energy conservation plan
- restoring an empty lot near our school to its original prairie condition
- winter illnesses (colds, flu) and how people could avoid spreading them
- keeping art and music programs in schools

Persuasive Letter

- why students in our school could benefit from a class in astronomy
- why the local science museum should organize an exhibit about local rock formations
- why the park district should plant more deciduous (or more evergreen) trees

portfolio

School–Home Connection

Keep a writing portfolio. Think about adding the activities from the *Practice the Strategy Notebook* to your writing portfolio. You may want to take your portfolio home to share.

EXPOSITORY writing

shares knowledge by presenting and explaining information.

1

Cause-and-Effect Report

2

Research Report

EXPOSITORY writing

Cause-and-Effect Report

This chapter will give you a chance to do one kind of expository writing, a **cause-and-effect report**.

A **cause-and-effect report** deals with the reasons or circumstances (**causes**) that lead to specific results or events (**effects**). Often, as with the samples in this chapter, the report focuses on a cause or causes that produce certain effects.

You will find a cause-and-effect report on the next page. First, read the questions below. Then read the report, keeping the questions in mind as you read.

 How clearly does the writer's thesis statement let the reader know the topic on which the paper will focus?

 How adequately does the writer select and organize effects that result from specific causes?

 How effectively does the writer use supporting details to show how a cause leads to a certain effect?

 How appropriately does the writer use transition words to emphasize cause-and-effect relationships?

 How carefully and correctly does the writer use apostrophes?

The Perils of Sleep Deprivation

by Dennis Nilssen

How much sleep a night is enough? Experts agree that just about everyone needs eight hours. And how long do most people sleep? The average is just less than seven hours. About one third of adults get less than six and a half. People may laugh off their sleep needs, saying that there aren't enough hours in the day to get everything done. But not getting enough sleep can harm a person's health and safety—as well as that of others—in many ways.

Did you ever hear the saying "A tired worker is only half a worker"? Everyone knows that sleepy workers can be a real problem in the workplace. They often get to work late. They don't contribute at meetings because they are too tired to pay attention. If they work with heavy equipment, they can easily injure themselves. If they are surgeons or pilots, they may botch surgeries or cause plane crashes. Consider the Chernobyl nuclear reactor accident and the Exxon Valdez oil spill. Both of these environmental catastrophes may have been the result of a worker not having enough sleep.

Some doctors think that constantly not getting enough sleep can damage a person's health. There is no conclusive proof yet, but certain tests have shown that sleep deprivation can strongly change people's metabolism. Biological and chemical processes in the body are affected. It may bring on diabetes. It may also trigger conditions related to old age in much younger people. Tests on sleep deprivation have also been done with laboratory rats. These have shown that the less sleep the animal gets, the less able it is to ward off infections. And the same may be true of humans.

The most dangerous sleepy person, however, may be the sleepy driver. This is because nearly 100,000 traffic accidents each year are at least partly caused by drowsy drivers. More than 1,500 people lose their lives each year in such accidents. And they are not just the drowsy drivers. They may also be passengers or other drivers that the sleepy person has hit.

Not getting enough sleep can clearly have terrible results. If you are a six-hours-a-night person, do yourself a favor. Start going to bed and getting up at reasonable times, and see how much better your days will be.

Using a Rubric

You know that a rubric is a tool that tells "what matters" in a piece of writing.

How do you use a rubric?
You assign 1, 2, 3, or 4 points to qualities in the writing. These points show how well the writer dealt with the various qualities.

The questions on page 188 were used to make this rubric.

Audience

How clearly does the writer's thesis statement let the reader know the topic on which the paper will focus?

Organization

How adequately does the writer select and organize effects that result from specific causes?

Elaboration

How effectively does the writer use supporting details to show how a cause leads to a certain effect?

Clarification

How appropriately does the writer use transition words to emphasize cause-and-effect relationships?

Conventions & Skills

How carefully and correctly does the writer use apostrophes?

> "Hello there! I'm Chantrelle, and I'm learning about cause-and-effect reports, too. What did you think of the report on page 189? Take a look at this rubric. Begin with the questions. Then read the information for each question. We'll use the rubric to evaluate the cause-and-effect report you just read."

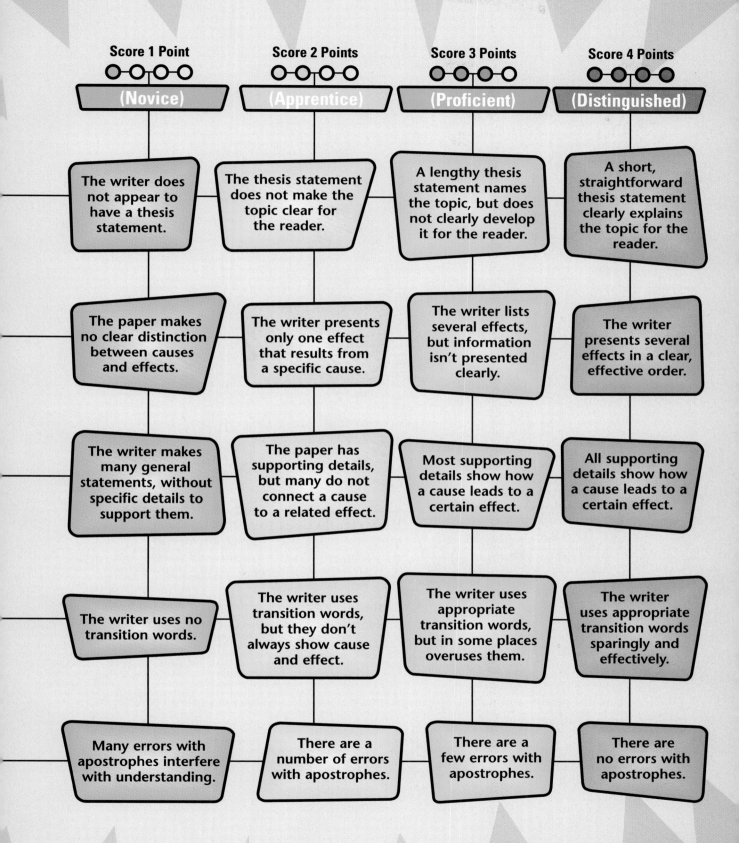

Score 1 Point (Novice)

The writer does not appear to have a thesis statement.

The paper makes no clear distinction between causes and effects.

The writer makes many general statements, without specific details to support them.

The writer uses no transition words.

Many errors with apostrophes interfere with understanding.

Score 2 Points (Apprentice)

The thesis statement does not make the topic clear for the reader.

The writer presents only one effect that results from a specific cause.

The paper has supporting details, but many do not connect a cause to a related effect.

The writer uses transition words, but they don't always show cause and effect.

There are a number of errors with apostrophes.

Score 3 Points (Proficient)

A lengthy thesis statement names the topic, but does not clearly develop it for the reader.

The writer lists several effects, but information isn't presented clearly.

Most supporting details show how a cause leads to a certain effect.

The writer uses appropriate transition words, but in some places overuses them.

There are a few errors with apostrophes.

Score 4 Points (Distinguished)

A short, straightforward thesis statement clearly explains the topic for the reader.

The writer presents several effects in a clear, effective order.

All supporting details show how a cause leads to a certain effect.

The writer uses appropriate transition words sparingly and effectively.

There are no errors with apostrophes.

Using a Rubric
to Study the Model

Discuss each question on the rubric with your classmates. Then use the rubric to evaluate Dennis Nilssen's cause-and-effect report on each question. Find sentences and paragraphs in it that help you answer each question.

Audience

How clearly does the writer's thesis statement let the reader know the topic on which the paper will focus?

" The writer put his thesis statement at the end of the first paragraph. Together with the lead-in he provided, it was very clear what topic he was going to be writing about. "

But not getting enough sleep can harm a person's health and safety—as well as that of others—in many ways.

How adequately does the writer select and organize effects that result from specific causes?

“ The writer deals with three general effects of not getting enough sleep—enough to build a good report around. He saved the one he thought was most serious—what happens on the road because of sleepy drivers—till last. Here are the effects of sleep deprivation he talked about. ”

Effect 1: hurts safety and productivity in the workplace
Effect 2: may harm health
Effect 3: creates unsafe drivers

How effectively does the writer use supporting details to show how a cause leads to a certain effect?

“ To make his points about effects, the author uses a lot of examples as supporting details. Take a look at this paragraph. The writer provides several supporting details and then adds real examples of bad things that happened because people didn't get enough sleep. ”

Did you ever hear the saying "A tired worker is only half a worker"? Everyone knows that sleepy workers can be a real problem in the workplace. They often get to work late. They don't contribute at meetings because they are too tired to pay attention. If they work with heavy equipment, they can easily injure themselves. If they are surgeons or pilots, they may botch surgeries or cause plane crashes. Consider the Chernobyl nuclear reactor accident and the Exxon Valdez oil spill. Both of these environmental catastrophes may have been the result of a worker not having enough sleep.

Clarification

How appropriately does the writer use transition words to emphasize cause-and-effect relationships?

> The writer uses words like **because** and **results** to tie causes and effects together. Here are two examples.

This is because nearly 100,000 traffic accidents each year are at least partly caused by drowsy drivers.

Not getting enough sleep can clearly have terrible results.

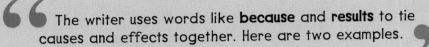

Conventions & Skills

How carefully and correctly does the writer use apostrophes?

> The writer uses apostrophes for contractions (aren't) and possessive nouns (people's)—not to form plurals.

. . . there aren't enough hours in the day . . .

. . . sleep deprivation can strongly change people's metabolism.

. . . they may botch surgeries or cause plane crashes.

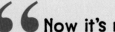 **Now it's my turn to write!**

I'm going to write a cause-and-effect report of my own. Watch me as I work. I'll be using the rubric and the model to help me practice good writing strategies.

ChanTrelle

Writer of a Cause-and-Effect Report

Name:	Chantrelle
Home:	Colorado
Hobbies:	hiking, skiing, crocheting, horseback riding
Favorite Book:	*Julie of the Wolves* by Jean Craighead George
Favorite Food:	fry bread
Assignment:	cause-and-effect report

Prewriting

Gather

Choose a condition in nature that causes certain effects. Do research and take notes about it.

> Because I live in a place that's pretty high up, I've had a chance to notice that the altitude can affect people who aren't used to it. I wondered if altitude could have the effect of actually making people sick, and if so, how seriously. Once I worked out this focus for my essay, I looked in science texts and Internet sites that I knew were reliable and appropriate. I found three specific effects of altitude. Here are the notes I took.

- less oxygen high up

- problems if people go too high too fast

  1. High Altitude Pulmonary Edema (fluid in lungs)
     - ◆ tightness in the chest, feeling of suffocation, cough
     - ◆ skin may turn colors, thinking becomes unclear, may even die
     - ◆ go down, seek medical help

  2. High Altitude Cerebral Edema (brain tissue swells, fluids leak)
     - ◆ loss of coordination, confused mental functions; could lead to death
     - ◆ happens after about a week at high altitude
     - ◆ come down right away, get treatment

  3. Acute Mountain Sickness (pretty common)
     - ◆ generally get it over 10,000 feet
     - ◆ headaches, dizziness, shortness of breath, sometimes nausea
     - ◆ usually feel better when get used to height

Go to page 96 in the **Practice** the Strategy **Notebook!**

Prewriting

Organize
Make a cause-and-effect chain to organize my notes.

> It was clear from my notes that I had enough information about effects of high altitudes. Because I was writing about cause and effect, it made sense to use a cause-and-effect chain to organize what I knew. The chain helped me figure out which effect I wanted to start and end with. I decided it made sense to start with the least serious effect, Acute Mountain Sickness, and work up.

Cause-and-Effect Chain

A **cause-and-effect chain** shows the reasons (causes) for specific events or results (effects). Sometimes several causes lead to one effect. In other cases, one cause has several effects. An effect can also become a cause of another effect.

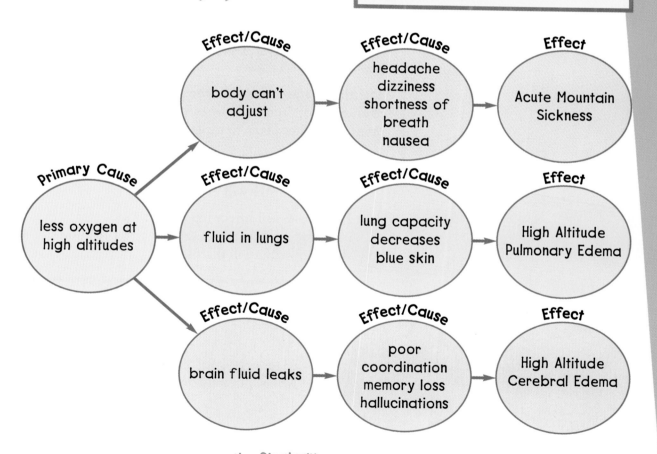

Effect/Cause
body can't adjust

Effect/Cause
headache
dizziness
shortness of breath
nausea

Effect
Acute Mountain Sickness

Primary Cause
less oxygen at high altitudes

Effect/Cause
fluid in lungs

Effect/Cause
lung capacity decreases
blue skin

Effect
High Altitude Pulmonary Edema

Effect/Cause
brain fluid leaks

Effect/Cause
poor coordination
memory loss
hallucinations

Effect
High Altitude Cerebral Edema

Go to page 98 in the **Practice the Strategy Notebook!**

Drafting

Write

Draft my report. Start by composing my thesis statement.

"I knew the main point I wanted to make in my report: that high altitudes can have serious effects on health. So I followed the **Rubric** and created a thesis statement to get that idea across. Once I did that, the rest of the report was fairly simple to organize. I decided to devote one paragraph to each of the three effects I had learned about.

"As I drafted, I concentrated on getting my ideas down. I did my best with spelling, capitalization, and grammar, but I didn't worry too much about them. I planned on carefully checking for errors later."

Thesis Statement

The **thesis statement** tells the purpose or main idea of an essay or report. A thesis statement clarifies the point the writer plans to explain or prove.

- Thesis statements usually come in the first paragraph, so that the audience understands the point the writer will be making.

- In a cause-and-effect report, the thesis statement focuses on the cause-and-effect relationship the writer will discuss.

What High Altitudes Can Do to You

Ive lived in high altitudes all of my life, so they don't bother me at all. However, when visitors come to stay at our loge they often have a hard time. There is less oxygen in the air up here, and some people have big problems adjusting to it. Sometimes, especially if they go out climbing, they really feel sick. By reading and observing, I've learned that high altitudes can have some pretty serius effects on people. ← **thesis statement**

One effect is something called Acute Mountain Sickness. When our guests hike up around 10,000 feet, this is mostly what they get. The symptoms they complain about include headaches, dizziness, shortness of breath, and sometimes nausea. Most of the time they are able to continue climbing. After a couple of days, they begin to get used to the heights. If they climb at a moderite pace, they are usually all right. But they have to be careful and not try to go too high too quickly. Otherwise, their conditions can get worse.

High Altitude Pulmonary Edema is another possible problem. As the lungs capacity decreases, people's skin may turn blue. If the edema isnt treated, people can die from it. They must go down from the high altitude and get medical help.

Another thing that can happen is High Altitude Cerebral Edema. About a week straight in high altitudes will do it. The brains fluids begin to leak out, and the brain tissue swells. There can be poor coordination, memory loss, and even hallucinations. These symptoms are noticed, and sufferers cant wait around; they must desend and see a doctor. Otherwise, death is possible.

Altitude sickness does not always cause serious problems. But people must be careful and observant when they are at heights they arent accustomed to.

Go to page 99 in the Practice the Strategy Notebook!

Revising

Elaborate

Make sure I have included enough supporting details to show how a cause leads to certain effects.

> " After I finished writing my first draft, I read it over to myself. I did what the **Rubric** said: made sure I had enough supporting details to show how effects were related to my cause. My first effect paragraph sounded okay, but I wasn't too happy with the second one. I put in a few more supporting details to make the effects clearer. "

Supporting Detail

A **supporting detail** is an example, anecdote, fact, or reason that supports a larger idea.

[2nd DRAFT]

supporting detail ⟶ The high altitude can cause fluid to develop in the lungs. This can prevent enough oxygen from getting into the blood.

High Altitude Pulmonary Edema is another possible problem. As the lungs capacity decreases, people's skin may turn blue. If the edema isnt treated, people can die from it. They must go down from the high altitude and get medical help.

supporting detail ⟶ Other possible effects of lessened lung capacity are coughing and chest tightness, or a feeling of suffocation.

Go to page 101 in the **Practice** the Strategy **Notebook!**

Revising

Clarify
Check to see that I have used transition words to make cause-and-effect relationships clear.

" The **Rubric** said to make cause-and-effect relationships clear with transition words. I knew that using too many could make my writing seem phony, but I thought adding a few to my third paragraph—and rewording as necessary—could make the information easier to understand. "

Transition Word

A **transition word** or phrase ties ideas together. It signals the reader that the writing is moving from one idea to another, usually related, idea.

- In a cause-and-effect report, these transition words and phrases are often found: *because, effect, so, since, therefore, as a result.*
- Other common transitions include words like the following: *after, while, then, first, second, third, next, before, once, also.*

[3rd DRAFT]

reage— *rewording*

A third possible effect of high altitudes

~~Another thing that can happen~~ is High Altitude Cerebral Edema. About

This condition usually comes after

a week straight in high altitudes ~~will do it~~. The brains fluids begin to

transition phrases

as a result

leak out, and the brain tissue swells. ~~There can be~~ poor coordination,

Once

memory loss, and even hallucinations. These symptoms are noticed, ~~and~~

sufferers cant wait around; they must desend and see a doctor.

Otherwise, death is possible.

rewording — Because the brain is affected, symptoms may include

Go to page 102 in the **Practice** the Strategy **Notebook!**

Expository Writing • Cause-and-Effect Report

201

Editing

Proofread

Make sure I've used apostrophes correctly in possessive nouns and contractions.

" The **Rubric** says to check for correct apostrophe use. I especially wanted to make sure that I didn't leave the apostrophes out of possessive nouns—something I sometimes do when I'm not thinking. I also wanted to make sure I didn't use apostrophes to make plurals. "

Apostrophes

Singular nouns and plural nouns that don't end in *s* form the possessive by adding *'s*.

friend—friend**'s**   James—James**'s**
men—men**'s**   children—children**'s**

Plural nouns ending in *s* form the possessive by adding an apostrophe.

trees—trees'   buses—buses'

An apostrophe replaces the missing letter or letters in a contraction.

do + not = don't   I + would = I'd
let + us = let's   it + is = it's

Do not use an apostrophe to form the possessive of *it*.

its paw (<u>not</u> it's paw)

Extra Practice
See **Apostrophes** (pages CS 18–CS 19) in the back of this book.

[4th DRAFT]

What High Altitudes Can Do to You

contraction

I've lived in high altitudes all of my life, so they don't bother me at all. However, when visitors come to stay at our loge they often have a hard time. There is less oxygen in the air up here, and some people have big problems adjusting to it.

High Altitude Pulmonary Edema is another possible problem. The high altitude can cause fluid to develop in the lungs. This can prevent enough oxygen from getting into the blood. As the lungs' capacity decreases, *plural possessive* people's skin may turn blue. Other possible effects of lessened lung capacity are coughing and chest tightness, or a feeling of suffocation. If the edema isn't treated, people can die from it. *contraction* They must go down from the high altitude and get medical help.

A third possible effect of high altitudes is High Altitude Cerebral Edema. This condition usually comes after about a week straight in high altitudes. The brain's fluids begin to leak out, and the brain tissue swells *singular possessive* as a result. Because the brain is affected, symptoms may include poor coordination, memory loss, and even hallucinations. Once these symptoms are noticed, sufferers can't wait around; they must descend *contraction* and see a doctor. Otherwise, death is possible.

Altitude sickness does not always cause serious problems. But people must be careful and observant when they're at heights that are unusual for them. *contraction*

Go to page 103 in the **Practice the Strategy Notebook!**

Publishing

Writer: Chantrelle

Assignment: cause-and-effect report

Topic: altitude sickness and its possible effects

Audience: anyone with Internet access

Method of Publication: post on school Web site

Reason for Choice: I liked my report because it talked about effects of altitude in an easy-to-understand way. It was also partially based on my own experience. I thought the information could be useful to other people.

66 Because I knew there would be a lot of people in my audience, I wanted my report to look and sound great. Here is what I did to get it ready. **99**

1. First, I checked my report to make sure I had corrected all errors.

2. I added my name and school information after the title of the report.

3. Next, I typed it up neatly.

4. I delivered the report to the person in charge of our Web site.

5. I recommended links to other sites that dealt with my topic, so that they could be built into my report.

What High Altitudes Can Do to You
by Chantrelle, Douglas Middle School

I've lived in high altitudes all of my life, so they don't bother me at all. However, when visitors come to stay at our lodge they often have a hard time. There is less oxygen in the air up here, and some people have big problems adjusting to it. Sometimes, especially if they go out climbing, they really feel sick. By reading and observing, I've learned that high altitudes can have some pretty serious effects on people.

One effect is something called Acute Mountain Sickness. When our guests hike up around 10,000 feet, this is mostly what they get. The symptoms they complain about include headaches, dizziness, shortness of breath, and sometimes nausea. Most of the time they are able to continue climbing. After a couple of days, they begin to get used to the heights. If they climb at a moderate pace, they are usually all right. But they have to be careful and not try to go too high too quickly. Otherwise, their conditions can get worse.

High Altitude Pulmonary Edema is another possible problem. The high altitude can cause fluid to develop in the lungs. This can prevent enough oxygen from getting into the blood. As the lungs' capacity decreases, people's skin may turn blue. Other possible effects of lessened lung capacity are coughing and chest tightness, or a feeling of suffocation. If the edema isn't treated, people can die from it. They must go down from the high altitude and get medical help.

A third possible effect of high altitudes is High Altitude Cerebral Edema. This condition usually comes after about a week straight in high altitudes. The brain's fluids begin to leak out, and the brain tissue swells as a result. Because the brain is affected, symptoms may include poor coordination, memory loss, and even hallucinations. Once these symptoms are noticed, sufferers can't wait around; they must descend and see a doctor. Otherwise, death is possible.

Altitude sickness does not always cause serious problems. But people must be careful and observant when they're at heights that are unusual for them.

USING the Rubric for Assessment

Go to pages 104–105 in the **Practice** the Strategy **Notebook!** Use that rubric to assess Chantrelle's report. Try using the rubric to assess your own writing.

EXPOSITORY writing

Research Report

This chapter will focus on a **research report,** one kind of expository writing.

A **research report** is an informational account in which the writer poses questions or raises issues, and then provides answers or explains discoveries. The writer gets information from several sources and identifies those sources at the end of the paper.

The piece of writing on the next three pages is a research report. Read these questions, and then read the report. Keep the questions in mind as you read.

 How successfully does the writer show awareness of the audience in presenting facts and ideas?

 How effectively does the writer introduce, develop, and then summarize the topic of the report?

 How accurately and appropriately has the writer quoted authorities and identified sources of information?

 How well has the writer summarized sources' ideas and presented them in his or her own words?

 How accurately are proper nouns, proper adjectives, and abbreviations capitalized and punctuated?

The Weight Problem in America

by Isabel Sandoval

Next time you're in a crowd, take a look around you. If the crowd is typical, many people probably are heavier than they should be. Weight has become a real health issue in America. This paper will present facts and discuss causes. It will also suggest possible ways to overcome our weight problem.

Are all overweight people unhealthy or unfit? No. Some heavy people are very fit. Muscular people weigh more than others who look about the same size. This is because muscle is heavier than fat. Pregnant women also weigh more than they would normally. Some people are just heavier than others. That doesn't always mean they are unhealthy. However, many people who are seriously overweight are at risk for health problems.

Here are some figures to think about. More than 97 million Americans are overweight. According to the American Obesity Association, about 39 million of these are obese. *Obese* means more than 30 pounds overweight. Obesity is the cause of some 300,000 deaths in this country every year. It is also a risk factor in many ailments. These include heart disease, arthritis, diabetes, high cholesterol, and cancer. According to U.S. Surgeon General David Satcher, obesity is "an epidemic."

Weight problems are not unknown in other countries. However, they are much easier to fall prey to in the United States. Consider Sam Moore, who moved here from Sierra Leone in 1998. His story is fairly common. "When I first came," Sam told writer Lawrence Lindner, "I was around 165 [pounds]. Now I'm looking at close to 200. It creeps up on you." Sam is 5 foot 9 inches tall. Two hundred pounds is definitely more than he should weigh.

Other immigrants report similar weight gain. Some of them were asked to think about why their weight shot up. Many pointed out the size of restaurant portions. Over and over, they talked about the size of meals served in American restaurants. One woman commented on a huge salad and enormous dish of pasta she was served for dinner. She noted that even her 6-foot 5-inch boyfriend couldn't have eaten it all. Yet the meal was a typical size for an American diner in a restaurant.

So the amount Americans eat is one part of the problem. Another problem is the kind of food Americans eat. In China, a meal might consist of a clear soup containing several vegetables. This would fill you up because of its high fiber and water content. However, it would not give you a lot of empty calories. Compare this sort of meal with a cheeseburger, French fries, and soft drink, an all-too-common American dinner. If you have a large-size portion of each, you would be taking in up to 1800 calories. Fast food restaurants, where you get most fattening meals like this, now account for 40 percent of the average family's food budget.

Besides eating large meals, Americans are also great snackers. It's no surprise that many popular snacks are fattening. For example, a 4-ounce bag of cheese puffs or potato chips contains 640 calories. A piece of cheesecake has about 470 calories. By contrast, an apple or a pear has fewer than 90 calories.

A final important part of the American weight problem is the amount of exercise people get. Generally speaking, it's far too little. For example, in 1991 nearly half of our schools had daily physical education classes. By 1997 only 27 percent did. More students watch TV or play video games after school than play sports. In a recent study by the Centers for Disease Control, only 28 percent of overweight adults who tried to exercise actually did so enough to make a difference. Many overweight adults did not exercise at all.

What can we do? One good piece of advice is this: Get a better understanding of what an appropriate portion is. In spite of what restaurants serve, the average eater doesn't need a serving-bowl portion of pasta. Nor should he or she return from the salad bar carrying a plate of nachos as well as lettuce. Some researchers consider knowledge of portions the most crucial help in losing weight.

If you are going to snack, snack sensibly. Read the labels on snack-food packages to see how many calories a serving contains. Beware of packages that don't give this information. And remember, unpackaged foods such as fruits and vegetables are the healthiest snacks of all.

Finally, exercise should be an important part of any plan to lose weight. The typical overweight adult should exercise 30 minutes a day, 5 days a week. Many people find it impossible to keep to that schedule. They should try to exercise three days a week at the very least.

Weight is a serious problem in America. It is not going to disappear quickly. However, many people can make real progress by following advice in this report. They will find that slimming down and becoming more fit is a healthier way to live.

Bibliography

Goff, Karen Goldberg. "Big, Bigger, SUPERBIG." Insight on the News 25 September 2000: 22.

Jibrin, Janis. The Unofficial Guide to Dieting Safely. New York: Macmillan, 1998.

Lindner, Lawrence. "It's a Big Country: When People Move to the U.S., They Get Fat. What Does This Tell Us About How We Eat?" The Washington Post 27 March 2001: T11.

"Obese Children." PBS. 1 May 2001 <http://www.pbs.org/newshour/bb/health/jan-june01/obesekids_05-01.html>.

"What Is Obesity?" American Obesity Association. 22 June 2000 <http://www.obesity.org/what.htm>.

Using a Rubric

A rubric is an evaluation tool that lists "what matters" for a piece of writing.

You know that to use a rubric you assign 1, 2, 3, or 4 points to qualities in a piece of writing to show how well the author dealt with them. The questions on page 206 were used to make this rubric.

" Hi! My name is Travis. I'm learning about writing research reports, too. What did you think of the report you just read? Read this rubric. Start with the questions. Then read the information for each question. We'll use the rubric to evaluate the research report. "

Audience

How successfully does the writer show awareness of the audience in presenting facts and ideas?

Organization

How effectively does the writer introduce, develop, and then summarize the topic of the report?

Elaboration

How accurately and appropriately has the writer quoted authorities and identified sources of information?

Clarification

How well has the writer summarized sources' ideas and presented them in his or her own words?

Conventions & Skills

How accurately are proper nouns, proper adjectives, and abbreviations capitalized and punctuated?

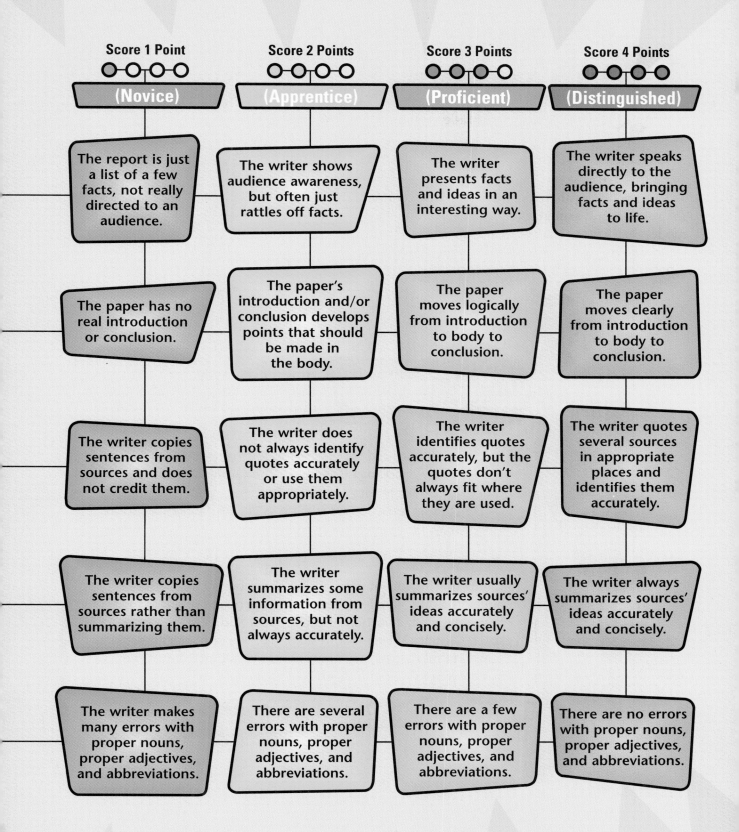

Score 1 Point

(Novice)

The report is just a list of a few facts, not really directed to an audience.

The paper has no real introduction or conclusion.

The writer copies sentences from sources and does not credit them.

The writer copies sentences from sources rather than summarizing them.

The writer makes many errors with proper nouns, proper adjectives, and abbreviations.

Score 2 Points

(Apprentice)

The writer shows audience awareness, but often just rattles off facts.

The paper's introduction and/or conclusion develops points that should be made in the body.

The writer does not always identify quotes accurately or use them appropriately.

The writer summarizes some information from sources, but not always accurately.

There are several errors with proper nouns, proper adjectives, and abbreviations.

Score 3 Points

(Proficient)

The writer presents facts and ideas in an interesting way.

The paper moves logically from introduction to body to conclusion.

The writer identifies quotes accurately, but the quotes don't always fit where they are used.

The writer usually summarizes sources' ideas accurately and concisely.

There are a few errors with proper nouns, proper adjectives, and abbreviations.

Score 4 Points

(Distinguished)

The writer speaks directly to the audience, bringing facts and ideas to life.

The paper moves clearly from introduction to body to conclusion.

The writer quotes several sources in appropriate places and identifies them accurately.

The writer always summarizes sources' ideas accurately and concisely.

There are no errors with proper nouns, proper adjectives, and abbreviations.

Using a Rubric
to Study the Model

With your classmates, discuss each question on the rubric. Find sentences and paragraphs in the model that help you answer each question. Then use the rubric to evaluate Isabel Sandoval's research report on each question.

Audience

How successfully does the writer show awareness of the audience in presenting facts and ideas?

"Throughout this paper I get the sense that the writer is talking directly to the audience. She uses a lot of facts and numbers, but she combines these with information presented in an interesting, engaging way, as in this paragraph."

Compare this sort of meal with a cheeseburger, French fries, and soft drink, an all-too-common American dinner. If you have a large-size portion of each, you would be taking in up to 1800 calories. Fast food restaurants, where you get most fattening meals like this, now account for 40 percent of the average family's food budget.

**Organization**

How effectively does the writer introduce, develop, and then summarize the topic of the report?

" The writer introduces the topic well, moves into facts and other information about it, and then has an effective ending. I particularly liked her introduction; it made me want to keep reading. "

Next time you're in a crowd, take a look around you. If the crowd is typical, many people probably are heavier than they should be. Weight has become a real health issue in America. This paper will present facts and discuss causes. It will also suggest possible ways to overcome our weight problem.

**Elaboration**

How accurately and appropriately has the writer quoted authorities and identified sources of information?

" The writer identifies formal sources such as the Centers for Disease Control and quotes informal ones such as Sam Moore. She also reports directly how the Surgeon General regards obesity. "

According to U.S. Surgeon General David Satcher, obesity is "an epidemic."

Clarification

How well has the writer summarized sources' ideas and presented them in his or her own words?

" Most of the writer's statistics about obesity in America come from the American Obesity Association's Web site. She uses her own words to present these pieces of information. "

More than 97 million Americans are overweight. According to the American Obesity Association, about 39 million of these are obese. *Obese* means more than 30 pounds overweight. Obesity is the cause of some 300,000 deaths in this country every year. It is also a risk factor in many ailments.

Conventions & Skills

How accurately are proper nouns, proper adjectives, and abbreviations capitalized and punctuated?

" The writer capitalizes proper nouns and abbreviations correctly. Here is an example of a citation for a magazine article. Notice how names and titles are capitalized. "

Lindner, Lawrence. "It's a Big Country: When People Move to the U.S., They Get Fat. What Does This Tell Us About How We Eat?" The Washington Post 27 March 2001: T11.

 Now it's my turn to write!

I'm going to write my own research report. Follow along to see how I use the model and also the rubric to help me practice good writing strategies. "

TRAVIS

Writer of a Research Report

Name:	Travis
Home:	Pennsylvania
Hobbies and Interests:	hiking with my family, collecting wild berries and other foods
Favorite Book:	*Carver: A Life in Poems* by Marilyn Nelson
Favorite Teacher:	my dad (a college professor and an expert on wild plants)
Assignment:	research report

Prewriting

Gather

Choose a topic and make a K-W-S chart. Get information from the Internet and other appropriate sources and record it on note cards.

"It was pretty easy for me to pick a research-report topic. I knew about foods growing in the wild from hikes with my dad, but I wondered what kinds of medicines come from plants and trees. I started by making a K-W-S (**K**now-**W**ant to Know-**S**ources) chart. Things I had already learned from Dad went in the first column. Things I wanted to know went in the second column. Then I started to research. As I found information, I noted the sources in the third column. I wrote just enough to remind me which book or article had answered each question."

What I Know	What I Want to Know	Sources to Answer My Questions
Many medicines are derived from plants.	How many?	Bierer, Carlson, King article
Quinine and digitalis are well-known medicines from plants.	How were these discovered? What are they used for?	Sumner book
Old tribal remedies are sometimes sources of medicines.	What are some examples?	Cox article
Tropical rain forests are home to many medicinal plants.	Why do so many grow there?	Bierer, Carlson, King article
Some people are looking at plants for cancer cures.	Has much progress been made?	article in Texas Medical Center News

Expository Writing • Research Report

> I found about five sources that seemed like they might be useful. As I went through each one, I followed the strategy of making note cards to record the information I found.
>
> "Here is one of the cards I made. I put the information in quotation marks because it is a direct quote from an article.

Note Card

A **note card** is a place, usually an index card, to put information about a topic. It should contain the following:

- a label identifying the topic
- information relating to the topic (either summarized or directly quoted)
- the source of the information

Use one note card for each source or piece of information.

label → Why rain forest is source of so many medicinal plants

quote → "Plants living in tropical forest habitats have had to develop and survive under intense competition for resources and nutrients. They have also had to develop an extraordinary array of defenses, most of them chemical, to protect themselves from viral diseases, fungal pathogens, insects and mammalian predators."

source → Bierer, Donald E., Thomas J. Carlson, and Steven R. King. "Shaman Pharmaceuticals: Integrating Indigenous Knowledge, Tropical Medicinal Plants, Medicine, Modern Science and Reciprocity into a Novel Drug Discovery Approach." NetSci's Science Center. May 1996 <http://www.netsci.org/Science/Special/index.html>.

Go to page 106 in the **Practice the Strategy Notebook!**

Prewriting

Organize

Make an outline to organize the information on my note cards. Distinguish between fact and opinion as I organize.

> When I finished my research, I had a lot of information on my note cards. To see if it all made sense together, I put the information into an outline to organize the body of my paper. I knew that a good topic outline would give me the basic structure, and I tried to be pretty specific with my words.
>
> "Most of the information that I gathered was facts—statements that can be proven to be true. I also had a few opinions mixed in—beliefs that cannot be proven to be true. To make sure that I didn't treat opinions in my paper as if they were facts, I labeled the opinions right on the outline.

Outline

An **outline** shows the main ideas and the supporting details of the paragraphs of an essay. A **topic outline** uses words and phrases to help a writer organize and arrange information. A **sentence outline** uses complete sentences. Use the same form for both outlines:

- Indicate major sections or topics with Roman numerals (e.g., I, II, III, IV).

- Indicate major paragraphs with capital letters (e.g., A, B, C).

- Indicate supporting details within each paragraph with Arabic numerals (e.g., 1, 2, 3).

- Use a period after each symbol.

- In a sentence outline, use the correct punctuation at the end of each sentence.

I. Some plant-based medicines around for many years ←——— **main idea**
   A. Quinine ←——— **paragraph topic**
      1. derived from bark of cinchona tree
      2. known about at least since 1600s ←——— **supporting details**
      3. treatment for malaria
   B. Digitalis
      1. derived from leaves of foxglove plant
      2. known about since 1700s, maybe earlier
      3. treatment for heart ailments (slows down pulse, regulates heartbeats)
   C. More than 120 plant-based medicines in use now
II. Some plant-based medicines found through new research
   A. Research with native peoples (Paul Alan Cox)
      1. interview with woman in Western Samoa
      2. information on more than 100 traditional remedies
      3. one remedy became basis for prostratin (used with AIDS patients)
   B. Research by scientists (Dr. Maktoob Alam)
      1. looking for cancer treatment
      2. has studied 200 rain-forest plants
      3. at least thirteen seem to block tumor cells
III. Rain forest problems must be overcome [OPINION]
   A. Fertile source of medicinal plants
      1. 25 percent of medicines come from there
      2. plants strong and effective because they compete to survive
   B. Ethical problems to overcome
      1. much information comes from native people
      2. need to pay these people [OPINION]
      3. long-term and short-term ways to pay
   C. Problem of disappearing rain forests
      1. about 150 acres per minute lost to development
      2. need to work out compromise with developing countries [OPINION]
         a. pay people for information
         b. pay people to help with research

Go to page 110 in the **Practice** the Strategy **Notebook!**

Drafting

Write   Draft my research report. Be sure to include a strong introduction, body, and conclusion.

" When I drafted the body of my research report, I tried to follow my outline as much as possible, because it reminded me what I wanted to include. I changed paragraph order just a little because some ideas came to me differently when I was actually writing. Because I had already thought about and outlined the body, I knew what I wanted to say in my introduction and conclusion. When I drafted my introduction and conclusion, I followed the strategy of making them as strong as possible.

"Getting my ideas down took a long time, so I didn't worry too much about spelling or capitalization as I drafted. I knew I could go back and fix any problems later. "

Introduction, Body, Conclusion

The **introduction** is the first paragraph of a paper. A good introduction grabs the audience's attention and states the topic or the point of the paper.

- In a **research report,** the introduction may give brief information or facts that lead up to or introduce the topic. The introduction usually tells aspects of the topic that the paper will cover.

The **body** is the main part of your writing. The body comes between the introduction and the conclusion and develops your main ideas about the topic.

- In a **research report,** the body may be 6–10 paragraphs long (or longer). The paragraphs discuss the topic mentioned in the introduction. Sources are quoted or summarized in your own words.

The **conclusion** is the last paragraph of a longer paper. The conclusion may tie up loose ends and summarize main ideas.

- In a **research report,** the conclusion may also look to the future. It may suggest ways to solve a problem or mention possible paths for additional research.

Modern Medicines From Ancient Plants

Most Americans know that many of our foods come from plants. Almost anyone can tell you that many berries grow on bushes. Many other fruits grow on trees, and many vegetables grow in the ground. It is not so well known, though, that a great number of medicines also come from plants. This paper will give some examples of plant-based medicines. It will talk about how they are discovered and how scientists learn about them. It will also explain why we need to be careful about how we treat areas that grow such plants.

Here is a number that might surprise you. According to research chemist Dr. Donald E. Bierer and his colleagues, "over 120 pharmaceutical products currently in use are plant-derived." This is more than 30 percent of our medicines. They include treatments for such things as malaria, heart problems, and Parkinson's disease.

One of the best-known plant-based medicines is quinine. Quinine comes from the bark of the cinchona tree. It is a standard treatment for malaria. Indians in south America have used the bark for centuries. It was brought to Europe in the 1600s. Before that, there was no effective malaria treatment there. As quinine became more commonly used, malaria was all but wiped out in many areas of the world.

Another widely used medicine is digitalis. Digitalis is derived from the leaves of the foxglove plant. Some say that it was used as long ago as 1500 B.C. We have records of it in sixteenth-century guides to herbs. In earlier times, it was used to treat swelling and wounds. Now it is used most often as a treatment for heart ailments. It slows down the pulse and regulates the heartbeat.

Quinine and digitalis are well-known plant-derived medicines. By talking to native people in remote areas, scientists are constantly learning about more medicinal plants. For example, one researcher interviewed body

an elderly woman in Western Samoa, an island in the pacific. Over several weeks, she gave him instructions on how to prepare more than 100 remedies. These were based on ferns and flowring plants. The National cancer Institute tested one of her preperations. It became the basis for a new antiviral drug called prostratin. This drug has been used in treating AIDS.

One area of great interest to researchers is anti-cancer drugs. Dr Maktoob Alam is a teacher at the University of Houston College of Pharmacy. He has screened about 200 rain-forest plants. In doing this, he has come up with 13 that seem to stop the functioning of cells in certain kinds of tumors. Other scientists are doing similar studies. The National Cancer Institute, for instance, continues to look for anti-cancer plants.

The tropical rain forests are a fertile source of medicinal plants. About 25 percent of medicines now on the market come from them. Many scientists think the rain forests are home to even more medicinal plants. Dr. Alam, for example, states that "the potential of finding an anti-cancer drug from them is greater than ever." What is the reason that so many of these plants may be in the rain forests? The answer is simple. Plants in these regions have had to develop an extraordinary array of defenses, most of them chemical, to protect themselves from viral diseases, fungal pathogens, insects and mammalian predators.

There are at least two problems associated with rain-forest research. One is an ethical one. Many of the plant remedies that researchers find come from native people, such as the Western samoan woman. By rights, such people should be paid for sharing their knowledge. It is not always easy to do this, however. Some native medicines may not be proven truly effective for years. Some may never be proven effective.

In the meantime, though, people could be paid in other ways. For example, they might receive healthcare, education facilities, or help starting rain-forest-friendly businesses.

The other problem is that the rain forests themselves are disappearing. According to some estimates, the world is losing about 150 acres of rain forest each minute. The reason is developement. As corporations clear the forests for timber, grazing lands, mining operations, and roadways, valuable plants are being destroyed. And once a plant species dissappears, it is gone forever.

It would be wonderful if a compromise could be worked out. Rain forests are much more valuable as they are than as grazing lands or roadways. Maybe local governments could invite more researchers and limit developers. Maybe, as dr. Brier suggests, local people could be paid for pointing out medicinal plants. Maybe they could be hired to work with scientists to help discover and study plants. In western Samoa, the government was promised half the income from prostratin. Perhaps this method can be used in other countries to keep the rain forest from disappearing.

According to some researchers, less than one percent of plant species have been thoroughly examined for their medicinal value. By saving as many of these as we can, who knows what remarkable cures we might find?

body

conclusion

Go to page 114 in the **Practice** the Strategy **Notebook!**

Revising

Elaborate
Add quotes and information from experts to help make important points.

> When I finished my first draft I had my partner, Josef, read it. He liked how I quoted Dr. Bierer and Dr. Alam, who are experts in the field of plant medicine. He thought I made a mistake in not citing a source for the story about the Western Samoan woman. So I went back and adjusted that paragraph.

READ TO A PARTNER

[2nd DRAFT]

expert cited ↓

Paul Alan Cox is director of the National Tropical Botanical Garden in Hawaii and Florida. He

Quinine and digitalis are well-known plant-derived medicines. By talking to native people in remote areas, scientists are constantly learning about more medicinal plants. For example, ~~one researcher~~ interviewed an elderly woman in Western Samoa, an island in the pacific. Over several weeks, she gave him instructions on how to prepare more than 100 remedies. These were based on ferns and flowring plants. The National cancer Institute tested one of her preperations. It became the basis for a new antiviral drug called prostratin. This drug has been used in treating AIDS.

> Because I included quotes and other information, I needed to cite my sources in a bibliography at the end of my report.

Citing Sources

When you **cite a source,** you tell readers where you found certain information. The examples below show how to present the information about a source in a bibliography. Pay attention to the order of the information and the use of commas, colons, and periods. Follow the rules for capitalization when creating a bibliography. In addition, use the styles shown here:

Book with one author:

> Tennenbaum, Lois. A Small Price to Pay. New York: Summit Company, 1999.

Book with two or three authors:

> Frunk, Francine, Marcul P. Mayberry, and Jane Quinn. The Life of Dr. Watts, Plant Researcher. West Ellis: Bonnie Press, 1995.

Signed newspaper or magazine article:

> Walkoee, Timothy. "Exploring the World in Your Backyard." Science Newsweekly 8 April 2001: 22.

Unsigned newspaper or magazine article:

> "Plants in the News." Crosstown Monthly September 2000: 38.

Web site with known author:

> Carlton, Sophie. "The Rain Forest." Ecology Federation. June 1998 <http://www.ecologyfederation.org/rainforest>.

Web site with unknown author:

> "Medicinal Plants." Science and You. 8 February 1997 <http://www.scienceandyou.com/medicinalplants1.html>.

Listings in a bibliography are arranged alphabetically according to the authors' last names. When there is no author, use the first word in the title.

Go to page 117 in the Practice the Strategy Notebook!

Revising

Clarify
Make sure that I have summarized accurately and not plagiarized information.

" Josef also noticed a place where the paper didn't sound like me at all, so he had me take a look at it. I quickly realized that I had quoted from an article without using quotation marks or telling who had made the statement. I was plagiarizing!

"To correct this mistake, I used the strategy of paraphrasing the information. I knew I would have to do a lot more than just change two or three words. I would have to restate the idea in a new sentence of my own. I decided to do this instead of quoting because I thought the sentence would be easier to understand if I put it in my own words. Read my change and see if I summarized the plagiarized sentence accurately. "

Paraphrase, Plagiarize

When a writer **paraphrases,** he or she restates another person's ideas in the writer's own words. When you paraphrase, you don't use quotation marks.

When a writer **plagiarizes,** he or she copies another writer's words and presents them as original. The actual writer is not cited. Plagiarizing is stealing another's words.

[3rd DRAFT]

The tropical rain forests are a fertile source of medicinal plants. About 25 percent of medicines now on the market come from them. Many scientists think the rain forests are home to even more medicinal plants. Dr. Alam, for example, states that "the potential of finding an anti-cancer drug from them is greater than ever." What is the reason that so many of these plants may be in the rain forests? The answer is simple. ~~Plants in these regions have had to develop an extraordinary array of defenses, most of them chemical, to protect themselves from viral diseases, fungal pathogens, insects and mammalian predators.~~

Rain-forest plants have had to find ways of defending themselves from diseases, funguses, animals, and insects. In doing so, they've strengthened themselves. ← **paraphrase**

Go to page 118 in the **Practice** the Strategy **Notebook!**

Expository Writing • Research Report   **227**

Editing

Proofread

Check capitalization and punctuation of proper nouns, proper adjectives, abbreviations, and initials.

66 Now I need to look for errors. The **Rubric** tells me to make sure proper nouns, proper adjectives, and abbreviations are correct. I'll also check my bibliography really well—looking closely at capitalization. 99

Proper Nouns, Proper Adjectives, and Abbreviations

Proper nouns name particular persons, places, and things. All important words in proper nouns are capitalized. **Initials** and **abbreviations** that are part of names are capitalized and followed by periods.

> Dr. Luz T. Lopez, M.D.
> Fell Company
> North Pole
> *The Call of the Wild* (book)

Proper adjectives are formed from proper nouns. They are capitalized.

> Danish cheese
> Latin American music
> Japanese cities
> French fries

Extra Practice

See **Proper Nouns, Proper Adjectives, and Abbreviations** (pages CS 20–CS 21) in the back of this book.

Proofreading Marks

⅂ Indent.	ℓ Take out something.
≡ Make a capital.	⊙ Add a period.
/ Make a small letter.	⌗ New paragraph
∧ Add something.	⑤Ⓟ Spelling error

It would be wonderful if a compromise could be worked out. Rain forests are much more valuable as they are than as grazing lands or roadways. Maybe local governments could invite more researchers and limit developers. Maybe, as dr. Brier suggests, local people could be paid for pointing out medicinal plants. Maybe they could be hired to work with scientists to help discover and study plants. In western Samoa, the government was promised half the income from prostratin. Perhaps this method can be used in other countries to keep the rain forest from disappearing.

According to some researchers, less than one percent of plant species have been thoroughly examined for their medicinal value. By saving as many of these as we can, who knows what remarkable cures we might find?

Bibliography

Bierer, Donald E., Thomas J. Carlson, and Steven r. King. "Shaman Pharmaceuticals: Integrating Indigenous Knowledge, Tropical Medicinal Plants, Medicine, Modern Science and Reciprocity into a Novel Drug Discovery Approach." NetSci's Science Center. May 1996 <http://www.netsci.org/Science/Special/index.html>.

Cox, Paul Alan. "Will Tribal Knowledge Survive the millennium?" <u>Science</u> 7 January 2000: 44.

Durand, Jennifer. "UH Professor Studies Rain Forest for Anti-Cancer Compound." Texas Medical Center. 1 March 1999 <http:/www.tmc.edu/tmcnews/3_01_99/page_13.html>.

Go to page 119 in the **Practice the Strategy Notebook!**

Publishing

Share

Present my report as part of a multimedia presentation to the class.

Writer: Travis

Assignment: research report

Topic: medicinal plants

Audience: classmates

Method of Publication: part of multimedia presentation

Reason for Choice: Some of my classmates had pictures and samples of medicinal plants from science class. I realized that my written report would go together well with the visual materials they had. I also knew of a video clip that would be a great addition to the presentation.

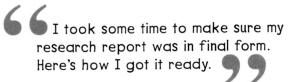

"I took some time to make sure my research report was in final form. Here's how I got it ready."

1. First, I read through my report again to be sure it had no errors.

2. Next, I doublechecked the spellings of names in the report and in my bibliography.

3. I typed my report on the computer.

4. I labeled my report with my name, my class, and the date.

5. Then, I put my report into a clear plastic binder.

6. I found the video clip about the rain forest.

7. Finally, I added my report and the video to the class presentation.

Travis
Science Class
January 15

Modern Medicines From Ancient Plants

Most Americans know that many of our foods come from plants. Almost anyone can tell you that many berries grow on bushes. Many other fruits grow on trees, and many vegetables grow in the ground. It is not so well known, though, that a great number of medicines also come from plants. This paper will give some examples of plant-based medicines. It will talk about how they are discovered and how scientists learn about them. It will also explain why we need to be careful about how we treat areas that grow such plants.

Here is a number that might surprise you. According to research chemist Dr. Donald E. Bierer and his colleagues, "over 120 pharmaceutical products currently in use are plant-derived." This is more than 30 percent of our medicines. They include treatments for such things as malaria, heart problems, and Parkinson's disease.

One of the best-known plant-based medicines is quinine. Quinine comes from the bark of the cinchona tree. It is a standard treatment for malaria. Indians in South America have used the bark for centuries. It was brought to Europe in the 1600s. Before that, there was no effective malaria treatment there. As quinine became more commonly used, malaria was all but wiped out in many areas of the world.

Another widely used medicine is digitalis. Digitalis is derived from the leaves of the foxglove plant. Some say that it was used as long ago as 1500 B.C. We have records of it in sixteenth-century guides to herbs. In earlier times, it was used to treat swelling and wounds. Now it is used most often as a treatment for heart ailments. It slows down the pulse and regulates the heartbeat.

Quinine and digitalis are well-known plant-derived medicines. By talking to native people in remote areas, scientists are constantly learning about more medicinal plants. For example, Paul Alan Cox is director of the National Tropical Botanical Garden in Hawaii and Florida. He interviewed an elderly woman in Western Samoa, an island in the Pacific. Over several weeks, she gave him instructions on how to prepare more than 100 remedies. These were based on ferns and flowering plants. The National Cancer Institute tested one of her preparations. It became the basis for a new antiviral drug called prostratin. This drug has been used in treating AIDS.

One area of great interest to researchers is anti-cancer drugs. Dr. Maktoob Alam is a teacher at the University of Houston College of Pharmacy. He has screened about 200 rain-forest plants. In doing this, he has come up with 13 that seem to stop the functioning of cells in certain kinds of tumors. Other scientists are doing similar studies. The National Cancer Institute, for instance, continues to look for anti-cancer plants.

The tropical rain forests are a fertile source of medicinal plants. About 25 percent of medicines now on the market come from them. Many scientists think the rain forests are home to even more medicinal plants. Dr. Alam, for example, states that "the potential of finding an anti-cancer drug from them is greater than ever." What is the reason that so many of these plants could be in the rain forests? The answer is simple. Rain-forest plants have had to find ways of defending themselves from diseases, funguses, animals, and insects. In doing so, they've strengthened themselves.

There are at least two problems associated with rain-forest research. One is an ethical one. Many of the plant remedies that researchers find come from native people, such as the Western Samoan woman. By rights, such people should be paid for sharing their knowledge. It is not always easy to do this, however. Some native medicines may not be proven truly effective for years. Some may never be proven effective. In the meantime, though, people could be paid in other ways. For example, they might receive healthcare, education facilities, or help starting rain-forest-friendly businesses.

The other problem is that the rain forests themselves are disappearing. According to some estimates, the world is losing about 150 acres of rain forest each minute. The reason is development. As corporations clear the forests for timber, grazing lands, mining operations, and roadways, valuable plants are being destroyed. And once a plant species disappears, it is gone forever.

It would be wonderful if a compromise could be worked out. Rain forests are much more valuable as they are than as grazing lands or roadways. Maybe local governments could invite more researchers and limit developers. Maybe, as Dr. Bierer suggests, local people could be paid for pointing out medicinal plants. They could be hired to work with scientists to help discover and study plants. In Western Samoa, the government was promised half the income from prostratin. Perhaps this method can be used in other countries to keep the rain forest from disappearing.

According to some researchers, less than one percent of plant species have been thoroughly examined for their medicinal value. By saving as many of these as we can, who knows what remarkable cures we might find?

Bibliography

Bierer, Donald E., Thomas J. Carlson, and Steven R. King. "Shaman Pharmaceuticals: Integrating Indigenous Knowledge, Tropical Medicinal Plants, Medicine, Modern Science and Reciprocity into a Novel Drug Discovery Approach." NetSci's Science Center. May 1996 <http://www.netsci.org/Science/Special/index.html>.

Cox, Paul Alan. "Will Tribal Knowledge Survive the Millennium?" Science 7 January 2000: 44.

Durand, Jennifer. "UH Professor Studies Rain Forest for Anti-Cancer Compound." Texas Medical Center. 1 March 1999 <http://www.tmc.edu/tmcnews/3_01_99/page_13.html>.

Sumner, Judith. The Natural History of Medicinal Plants. Portland, Oregon: Timber Press, 2000.

USING the Rubric for Assessment

Go to pages 120–121 in the **Practice** the Strategy **Notebook!** Use that rubric to assess Travis's report. Try using the rubric to assess your own writing.

your own
EXPOSITORY
writing
Social Studies

Put the strategies you practiced in this unit to work to write your own cause-and-effect essay, research report, or both! You can:

- develop the writing you did in the Your Own Writing pages of the *Practice the Strategy Notebook*;
- pick an idea below and write something new;
- choose another idea of your own.

Be sure to follow the steps in the writing process. Use the rubrics in this unit to assess your writing.

Cause-and-Effect Essay

- how air-conditioning changed America
- how industrialization changed conditions in Europe in the nineteenth century
- how the development of unions changed the lives of workers

Research Report

- what life was like around A.D. 1000 in Northern Europe
- great ancient empires of Africa (for example, Ghana or Mali)
- famous women in aviation history

portfolio

School–Home Connection

Keep a writing portfolio. Think about adding the activities from the *Practice the Strategy Notebook* to your writing portfolio. You may want to take your portfolio home to share.

TEST writing

A writing test measures how well you can organize your ideas.

Test Writing

- ☑ starts with a writing prompt.
- ☑ may not let writers use outside sources.
- ☑ may have a time limit.
- ☑ may not allow writers to recopy.

TEST writing

Analyze the Writing Prompt

Every writing test starts with a writing prompt. Even though they aren't labeled, most writing prompts have three parts: the Setup, the Task, and the Scoring Guide. Read the writing prompt below carefully. Can you find the Setup, the Task, and the Scoring Guide?

The parent-teacher group at your school has proposed a Turn-Off-the-TV Week for the students in your school.

Write a persuasive essay for your teacher telling why you support or oppose this plan. Be sure your writing

- clearly states your opinion for your reader.
- is well organized. You should state a point of view, give a new reason in each paragraph, and restate your opinion.
- includes facts or examples to support each reason.
- leaves out confusing or unnecessary ideas so that reasons are sound and to the point.
- uses the conventions of language and spelling correctly.

Most writing prompts have three parts:

This part of the writing prompt gives you the background information you need to get ready for writing.

The parent-teacher group at your school has proposed a Turn-Off-the-TV Week for the students in your school.

This part of the writing prompt tells you exactly what you're supposed to write.

Write a persuasive essay for your teacher telling why you support or oppose this plan.

This section tells how your writing will be scored. To do well on the test, you should include everything on the list.

Be sure your writing
- clearly states your opinion for your reader.
- is well organized. You should state a point of view, give a new reason in each paragraph, and restate your opinion.
- includes facts or examples to support each reason.
- leaves out confusing or unnecessary ideas so that reasons are sound and to the point.
- uses the conventions of language and spelling correctly.

Using the
Scoring Guide
to Study the Model

"Hi. I'm Ramon. Just like you, I have to write when I take a test sometimes. When that happens, I pay close attention to the Scoring Guide in the writing prompt.

"Do you remember the rubrics you've been using in this book? Each one told you what a piece of writing needs to be considered **Novice, Apprentice, Proficient,** or **Distinguished**.

"When you write on a test, you don't always have all that information handy. You just have the basics. However, the rubrics you've been using in this book have helped you learn how to pay attention to the most important areas in your writing: **Audience, Organization, Elaboration, Clarification,** and **Conventions & Skills**."

"On the next page, you can see what one student wrote in response to the writing prompt on page 236. You can tell that the student tried to keep the Scoring Guide in mind as she wrote! After you read this essay, we'll use the Scoring Guide in the writing prompt to check and see how well she did."

Turn It Off? No Way!
by Leah Alexander

If my school planned to have a Turn-Off-the-TV Week, I would be the first to protest. There are several reasons why I feel this way.

First of all, television is an excellent way of discovering what is going on in the world. Others might disagree and say that you can always read a news magazine or the newspaper instead of watching TV. Even so, sometimes there is important news that changes almost from minute to minute. For example, in the 2000 presidential election, people did not know which candidate had gotten more votes. For several weeks, TV was the best source of up-to-date information. Besides, you've heard that a picture is worth a thousand words? You just don't get the same kind of visual experience from other media.

Another reason for watching TV is that sometimes we kids need a break. After spending an hour on the school bus, six hours in school, and a couple of hours doing homework (not to mention an hour or two of sports and after-school clubs), we need some time off! I can't think of anything more relaxing than a good sitcom. That doesn't mean I would watch TV all night. I'm the first one to pick up a good book in my free time. I just think it's important not to work so hard all the time.

There is a third reason I don't support a week without television. I want to be an actress when I grow up. I think it's really helpful to watch both good and bad actors to see how—and how not—to act. Some people might say I should just go to the movies, but they are too expensive for me to spend my allowance on. Since television is usually free, you don't waste your money even if the show isn't very good.

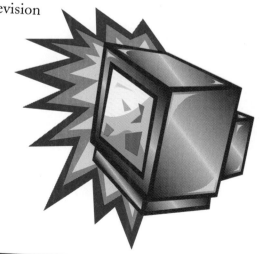

I can see skipping a night of TV now and then. I do it myself, especially if I have to study for a big test. A whole week without television seems like overkill.

I have no doubt that there are many reasons why people support the idea of a week of no television for kids. I just think, for responsible students like me, the reasons NOT to turn off the TV outweigh them.

" Look at each point on the Scoring Guide. Then look at what Leah wrote. See if you can find examples to show how well her essay did on each part of the Scoring Guide. **"**

Scoring Guide

The writer clearly states an opinion for the reader.

Audience

" Leah states her point of view in her opening sentence. It's pretty clear that she does not support the idea of a Turn-Off-the-TV Week. **"**

If my school planned to have a Turn-Off-the-TV Week, I would be the first to protest.

" I also notice that everything Leah wrote after that supports her point of view. Her opinion is very clear, and she never wavers from it. **"**

The paper is well organized. The writer states a point of view, gives a new reason in each paragraph, and restates the opinion.

Organization

"The writer begins her essay by explaining how she feels about the idea of a week with no TV. Then she gives reasons to support her point of view. Each paragraph in the body of her essay has a topic sentence that gives a new reason."

There is a third reason I don't support a week without television. I want to be an actress when I grow up. I think it's really helpful to watch both good and bad actors to see how—and how not—to act.

"The writer restates her opinion in the concluding paragraph. That helps readers remember just where she stands on the issue."

I have no doubt that there are many reasons why people support the idea of a week of no television for kids. I just think, for responsible students like me, the reasons NOT to turn off the TV outweigh them.

The writer includes facts or examples to support each reason.

Elaboration

"Leah gives facts to support her reason for saying that a TV-free week is not a good idea. Using facts is a good way to persuade an audience."

For example, in the 2000 presidential election, people did not know which candidate had gotten more votes. For several weeks, TV was the best source of up-to-date information.

The writer leaves out confusing or unnecessary ideas so that reasons are sound and to the point.

Clarification

"Information that is confusing or unnecessary distracts readers from the main points you are trying to make. This extra information weakens your argument. In the clarification step, you should take out any details that are confusing or unnecessary. This helps you make sure your reasons are sound and to the point, so your writing is more persuasive.

"In an earlier draft, Leah had written a sentence. She realized that it did not support her main reasons, and she deleted it."

There is a third reason I don't support a week without television. I want to be an actress when I grow up. I think it's really helpful to watch both good and bad actors to see how—and how not—to act. ~~You can see examples of really bad acting on some of the soap operas that my Aunt Penny watches.~~ Some people might say I should just go to the movies, but they are too expensive for me to spend my allowance on.

The writer uses the conventions of language and spelling correctly.

Conventions & Skills

"As far as I can see, Leah did not make any serious mistakes in capitalization, punctuation, sentence structure, or spelling. Check out these sentences. Do you see any mistakes? I say Leah did a good job."

Another reason for watching TV is that sometimes we kids need a break. After spending an hour on the school bus, six hours in school, and a couple of hours doing homework (not to mention an hour or two of sports and after-school clubs), we need some time off! I can't think of anything more relaxing than a good sitcom.

Now it's my turn to take a writing test.

Let's take a look at another writing prompt and see how well I do!

RamoN

Test Writing Champ

Name:	Ramon
Favorite Subject:	art
Favorite Book:	*Following Fake Man* by Barbara Ware Holmes
Hobbies:	sending e-mail to my buddies, playing with my dog
Assignment:	a persuasive essay for a test

PreWriting

Gather

Read and analyze the writing prompt. Make sure I understand what I am supposed to do.

" Let's look together at a piece of writing I am doing for a test. That will help you work on your own writing test strategies. Of course, the first thing writers do when they write is gather ideas. When you write to take a test, you start gathering information from the writing prompt.

"It's really important to read the writing prompt carefully because it will probably have three parts. The parts aren't labeled for you. You need to find the Setup, the Task, and the **Scoring Guide** yourself! You've got to find and think about all the parts and be sure you know exactly what you're supposed to do.

"Here's the writing prompt I have: "

Setup
> You believe that a special holiday should be created to honor a particular person or event. Think about a person or event that is important enough to you to be honored in this way.

Task
> Write an essay to persuade others that this person or event should be honored. Be sure your writing

Scoring Guide
> - clearly states your opinion for your reader.
> - is well organized. You should state a point of view, give a new reason in each paragraph, and restate your opinion.
> - includes facts or examples to support each reason.
> - leaves out confusing or unnecessary ideas so that reasons are sound and to the point.
> - uses the conventions of language and spelling correctly.

> Before I do anything else, I take the first five minutes to really study the writing prompt. I follow these steps so I know what to do:

1 Read all three parts of the prompt carefully.

> Okay! I found and read the **Setup,** the **Task,** and the **Scoring Guide** .

2 Circle key words in the Task part of the prompt that tell what kind of writing I need to do and who my audience is.

> I'll circle the words **essay to persuade**. That means I'm supposed to write my opinion about something and then try to convince my reader to agree with me and maybe even do something about it.
> "I'll also circle the words **person or event should be honored** because that's my topic. Part of this task will be actually choosing the important person or event I want to honor. The writing prompt doesn't say who my audience is, so I'll write my essay to my teacher.

3 Make sure I know how I'll be graded.

> The **Scoring Guide** part tells what I need to include in my writing. I need to pay close attention to this because that is how I'll get a good score!

4 Put what I need to do in my own words.

> Here's what I need to do: I need to persuade my reader that the person or event I choose should be honored with a special holiday.

Go to page 122 in the **Practice** the Strategy **Notebook!**

Prewriting

Organize   **Plan my time.**

" Prewriting is a little different when you take a test. You need to keep an eye on the clock! Think about how much time you have and divide the time into the different parts of the writing process. If I have one hour to finish the test, here's how I organize my time. "

Analyze the prompt
5 minutes

Edit
5 minutes

Revise
10 minutes

Prewrite
15 minutes

Draft
25 minutes

Prewriting
Gather and Organize

Choose a graphic organizer. Use it to organize my ideas.

"Because of the time limit, I have to think fast. My first task is to decide on my topic. Who do I know that should be honored with a special holiday? While I could write about my mom, I bet a lot of kids will write about family members. I know! I'm going to write about the veterinarian who saved my dog's life!

"I'll gather ideas and organize them at the same time. Since I'm writing a persuasive essay, a persuasion map will help me the most. (To review persuasion maps, see page 175.) I'll use the Setup and Task sections of the writing prompt as my Call to Action. The Scoring Guide tells me I need to include reasons, facts, and examples. The persuasion map will help me organize them."

Facts/Examples

Reason 1
Dr. Lamb saved my dog's life.

She performed surgery after he ate a necktie.

She gave up her evening out.

She flies to Central America to give free pet services.

Reason 2
Dr. Lamb cares for pets whose owners can't pay her.

She runs a pet clinic in her neighborhood.

She charges only $5.00 for a visit.

Reason 3
Everyone likes Dr. Lamb because she really cares about pets and people.

She came to Career Day at school.

People send her cards and thank-you notes.

Call to Action
Make a holiday to honor Dr. Lamb.

Prewriting

Organize
Check my graphic organizer against the Scoring Guide.

"In a test, you don't always get much time to revise. So prewriting is more important than ever! Even before I write, I'll check the information in my persuasion map against the **Scoring Guide** in the writing prompt."

Scoring Guide Be sure your writing clearly states your opinion for your reader.

"I'm going to write about why I think Dr. Lamb deserves to be honored with a special holiday. My call to action clearly states my opinion."

Call to Action
Make a holiday to honor Dr. Lamb.

Scoring Guide Be sure your writing is well organized. You should state a point of view, give a new reason in each paragraph, and restate your opinion.

"I'll begin by stating that Dr. Lamb should be honored. Then I'll write my paragraphs. I've already set up my persuasion map with three good reasons, so I'll write three paragraphs. I'll use my reasons as topic sentences."

Reason 1
Dr. Lamb saved my dog's life.

Reason 2
Dr. Lamb cares for pets whose owners can't pay her.

Reason 3
Everyone likes Dr. Lamb because she really cares about pets and people.

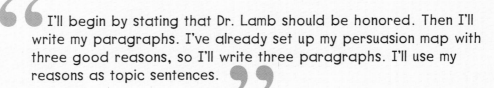

"I'll restate my opinion and give my call to action in my closing paragraph."

Be sure your writing includes facts or examples to support each reason.

" In my persuasion map, I've already jotted down facts and examples for each of my three reasons. (That persuasion map is really handy!) I'll use them to make up my paragraphs. They will follow my topic sentences, my reasons. "

Reason 1
Dr. Lamb saved my dog's life.

Facts/Examples
She performed surgery after he ate a necktie.

She gave up her evening out.

 Be sure your writing leaves out confusing or unnecessary ideas so that reasons are sound and to the point.

" I know it's easy to get off track or say too much when you're under pressure. I'll be extra careful to stay focused and stick to the point. "

 Be sure your writing uses the conventions of language and spelling correctly.

" I know to watch my spelling, grammar, capitalization, and punctuation. I don't want to leave any mistakes in my paper. "

" I think I'm in good shape and ready to write! "

Go to page 123 in the **Practice ∧ Notebook!**
                              the Strategy

Drafting

Write   Use my persuasion map to write a persuasive essay with reasons, facts, and examples.

" As I wrote, I checked my persuasion map to follow the organization. Here's what I wrote. I left room for corrections. "

[DRAFT]

Dr. Kitty Lamb Day

by Ramon

opinion

The person I would ~~name~~ nominate to be ~~a hero~~ honored with a special holiday is Dr. Kitty Lamb, our veterinarian. Believe it or not, that's her real name.) Dr. Lamb has been my dog's doctor since he was a pup. There are several reasons why I think Dr. Lamb is a real hero.

facts and examples

Reason 1 → The first reason is personal, since she saved my dog's life. Cato has been known to chew on many things that were not meant to be dog food. He once ~~ate~~ consumed the tire on my bicycle. The time he ~~sure~~ really got into trouble, however, was when he swallowed one of my dad's neckties. After he stopped eating and wouldn't stop groaning, we called Dr. Lamb. She said to bring Cato right over. When we got there she was all dressed up, because her and her husband were on there way to a party. She had to perform surgery for five ours to save that silly dog's life. After a few weeks Cato was completely recovered.

Reason 2 → The second reason I think Dr. lamb should be recognized is the volunteer work that she do. Every year, she flies to Central America with a group of other veterinarian's. There the doctors care for the pets of people who do not have enough money to pay for these services. One of the jobs they do is ~~like~~ perform surgery, so the animals won't have puppies or kittens that no one can care for. Even at home, Dr. Lamb helps people and their pets. Once a month, she runs a pet clinic here in town, where you can have your pet examined for just five dollars.

Reason 3 ——⟶

The last reason I think Dr. Lamb is a hero is the way she treats everyone—both animals and people. She came to our school on Career Day to tell about the work she does. If you ever visited her office. You would be amazed at all the cards and letters on her bulletin board. These are all thank-you notes from the owners of pets she has helped. She also has some pretty interesting magazines, but since you don't usually have to wait to see her, you may not get to read them.

facts and examples

I am so impressed by Dr. Lamb that I would like to become a veterinarian when I grow up. Since she is such an animal lover, I think a great way to honor her would be to hold a pet parade on the street in front of her office. She could wear a crown that says Top Dog, or something like that. Although there are many other heroes who you might think deserve a holiday of their won, Dr. Lamb gets my vote.

call to action

Be Neat!

" Remember, you may not get a chance to recopy your paper in a writing test. I tried to be neat when I wrote. "

Go to page 124 in the **Practice** the Strategy **Notebook!**

Revising

Elaborate

Check what I have written against the Scoring Guide. Add any missing facts or examples.

66 In a test, I can't read my paper to a partner, so I'll read it to myself. I'll keep the **Scoring Guide** at hand so I can check my paper against it. For this test, the **Scoring Guide** tells me to include facts and examples to support each of my reasons. I need to make sure I included enough information to convince my reader to agree with me about Dr. Lamb.

"After rereading I decided to add more facts and examples about Dr. Lamb's volunteer work. I think that section will be more persuasive now. 99

[DRAFT]

The second reason I think Dr. lamb should be recognized is the volunteer work that she do. Every year, she flies to Central America with a group of other veterinarian's. There the doctors care for the pets of people who do not have enough money to pay for these services. One of the jobs they do is ~~like~~ perform surgery, so the animals won't have puppies or kittens that no one can care for. Even at home, Dr. Lamb helps people and their pets. Once a month, she runs a pet clinic here in town, where you can have your pet examined for just five dollars.

added facts/examples → The doctors don't get paid for the work they do there. They even pay for their own plane tickets to get there.

Go to page 126 in the **Practice** the Strategy **Notebook!**

Revising

Clarify
Check what I have written against the Scoring Guide. Make sure everything is clear.

66 I'll read my paper to myself again. I'll check the **Scoring Guide** and make sure everything is clear.

"Look at the **Scoring Guide**. It says I need to make sure that my reasons are sound and that I stick to the point. From my rereading, I see I need to cross out some unnecessary information. 99

READ TO MYSELF

[DRAFT]

The last reason I think Dr. Lamb is a hero is the way she treats everyone—both animals and people. She came to our school on Career Day to tell about the work she does. If you ever visited her office. You would be amazed at all the cards and letters on her bulletin board. These are all thank-you notes from the owners of pets she has helped. She also has some pretty interesting magazines, but since you don't usually have to wait to see her, you may not get to read them.

↖ unnecessary information

66 This sentence about magazines has nothing to do with the reason I'm giving in this paragraph, so I took it out. 99

Go to page 127 in the **Practice** the Strategy **Notebook!**

Test Writing **253**

Editing

Proofread — Check that I have used correct grammar, capitalization, punctuation, and spelling.

66 It's a good idea to always check your paper one last time. The **Scoring Guide** says to use correct grammar, capitalization, punctuation, and spelling. I always leave plenty of time to check for errors in these important areas.

"We've seen checklists like the one below so often that I think of things on the lists automatically. Sometimes when I write something wrong now, it stands out. I notice it right away because I've started using the checklist in my head. 99

Proofreading Checklist

- ☑ Do all the sentences have a subject and verb?
- ☑ Do the subjects and verbs agree?
- ☑ Does each sentence begin with a capital letter and end with the correct punctuation?
- ☑ Have sentences been joined with a comma and a joining word or with a semicolon?
- ☑ Have commas been used correctly?
- ☑ Have double negatives been avoided?
- ☑ Have adjectives and adverbs been used correctly?
- ☑ Do all proper nouns begin with a capital letter?
- ☑ Have the correct subject and object pronouns been used?
- ☑ Have the possessive forms of nouns been formed correctly?
- ☑ Are all words spelled correctly?

Extra Practice
See **Review** (pages CS 22–CS 23) in the back of this book.

Proofreading Marks

⊐ Indent.

≡ Make a capital.

/ Make a small letter.

∧ Add something.

ℓ Take out something.

⊙ Add a period.

⌗ New paragraph

ⓢⓟ Spelling error

[DRAFT]

Dr. Kitty Lamb Day
by Ramon

The person I would ~~name~~ nominate to be ~~a hero~~ honored with a special holiday is Dr. Kitty Lamb, our veterinarian. (Believe it or not, that's her real name.) Dr. Lamb has been my dog's doctor since he was a pup. There are several reasons why I think Dr. Lamb is a real hero.

The first reason is personal, since she saved my dog's life. Cato has been known to chew on many things that were not meant to be dog food. He once ~~ate~~ consumed the tire on my bicycle. The time he ~~sure~~ really got into trouble, however, was when he swallowed one of my dad's neckties. After he stopped eating and wouldn't stop groaning, we called Dr. Lamb. She said to bring Cato right over. When we got there she was all dressed up, because ~~her~~ she and her husband were on ~~there~~ their way to a party. She had to perform surgery for five ~~ours~~ hours to save that silly dog's life. After a few weeks, Cato was completely recovered.

The second reason I think Dr. lamb should be recognized is the volunteer work that she ~~do~~ does. Every year, she flies to Central America with a group of other veterinarians. There the doctors care for the pets of people who do not have enough money to pay for these services. One of the jobs they do is ~~like~~ perform surgery, so the animals won't have puppies or kittens that no one can care for. Even at home, Dr. Lamb helps people and their pets. Once a month, she runs a pet clinic here in town, where you can have your pet examined for just five dollars. The doctors don't get paid for the work they do there. They even pay for their own plane tickets to get there.

The last reason I think Dr. Lamb is a hero is the way she treats everyone—both animals and people. She came to our school on Career Day to tell about the work she does. If you ever visited her office, You would be amazed at all the cards and letters on her bulletin board. These are all thank-you notes from the owners of pets she has helped. ~~She also has some pretty interesting magazines, but since you don't usually have to wait to see her, you may not get to read them.~~

I am so impressed by Dr. Lamb that I would like to become a veterinarian when I grow up. Since she is such an animal lover, I think a great way to honor her would be to hold a pet parade on the street in front of her office. She could wear a crown that says Top Dog, or something like that. Although there are many other heroes who you might think deserve a holiday of their own won, Dr. Lamb gets my vote.

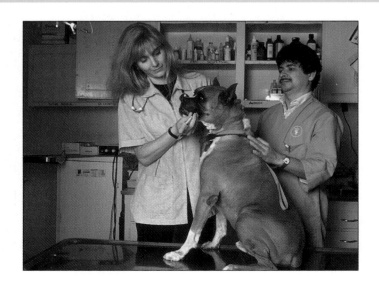

Go to page 128 in the Practice the Strategy Notebook!

We're finished! That wasn't so bad! The main thing to remember is that when you write for a test, you use the writing process. It's just a little different from other writing. Remember these important steps when you write for a test.

1. **Analyze the writing prompt before you start to write.**
   Most writing prompts have three parts: the Setup, the Task, and the Scoring Guide. The parts will probably not be labeled. You have to figure them out yourself!

2. **Make sure you understand the task before you start to write.**
   - Read all three parts of the writing prompt carefully.
   - Circle key words in the Task part of the prompt that tell what kind of writing you need to do. The Task might also identify your audience.
   - Make sure you know how you'll be graded.
   - Say the assignment in your own words to yourself.

3. **Keep an eye on the clock.**
   Decide how much time you will spend on each part of the writing process and try to stick to your schedule. Do not spend so much time on prewriting that you do not have any time left to write!

4. **Reread your writing. Check it against the Scoring Guide at least twice.**
   Remember the rubrics we have used all year? A Scoring Guide on a writing test is like a rubric. It can help you keep what is important in mind.

5. **Plan, plan, plan!**
   You do not get much time to revise during a test, so planning is more important than ever.

6. **Write neatly.**
   Remember, if the people who score your test cannot read your writing, it does not matter how good your story or report is!

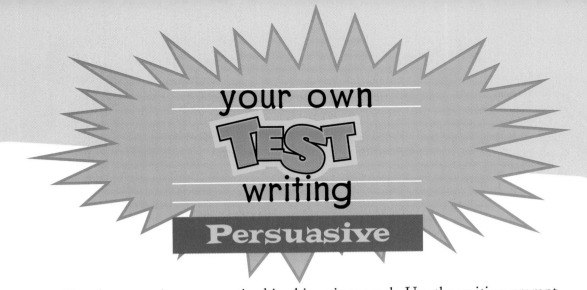

your own
TEST
writing
Persuasive

Put the strategies you practiced in this unit to work. Use the writing prompt below to take your own persuasive writing test. Pretend this is a real test and give yourself one hour to complete all of the steps. Use the Scoring Guide to evaluate your paper.

In some states, lawmakers are deciding whether students should be required to take physical education classes. How do you feel? Write a persuasive essay to support your point of view. Be sure your writing
• clearly states your opinion for your reader.
• is well organized. You should state a point of view, give a new reason in each paragraph, and restate your opinion.
• includes facts or examples to support each reason.
• leaves out confusing or unnecessary ideas so that reasons are sound and to the point.
• uses the conventions of language and spelling correctly.

portfolio

School–Home Connection

Keep a writing portfolio. Think about adding the activities from the *Practice the Strategy Notebook* to your writing portfolio. You may want to take your portfolio home to share.

Extra Practice

Conventions & SKILLS

The activities on the following pages provide additional practice in the grammar, usage, and mechanics skills you worked with throughout this book. Use the activities to get extra practice in these skills. Complete each activity on a separate sheet of paper.

Table of Contents

A correctly written sentence has a subject and a predicate and expresses a complete thought. A **fragment** is a group of words that begins with a capital letter and ends with a period or other end punctuation but does not state a complete thought.

A **run-on sentence** is two simple sentences that are run together and are not correctly joined by a correct joining word or punctuation.

ReView the Rule

Correct a sentence fragment in one of these ways.

- Add a subject, a predicate, or both.
- Attach the fragment to a related sentence.

Correct a run-on sentence in one of these ways.

- Combine the sentences with both a comma and a conjunction such as *and*, *but*, *or*, or *for*.
- Combine the sentences with a semicolon.
- Write two separate sentences.

Practice

Now let's put what you learned to use. Number your paper from 1.–25. Rewrite each incorrect sentence and correct each fragment and run-on. If a sentence is correct, write **Sentence**.

1. Architecture, a topic of interest to many people.

2. Very high structures are particularly fascinating.

3. The very earliest skyscrapers in the 1880s.

4. City real estate was very expensive, it was cheaper to build up than to build out.

5. The invention of the elevator made tall buildings possible.

6. "Tall" in the early days meaning only ten or twelve stories high.

7. Some call Chicago the home of the skyscraper others say New York.

8. The Home Reliance Building was constructed in Chicago in 1885.

9. Some people were frightened, they thought the building might topple over.

10. Many technical advances in the early twentieth century.

11. The Woolworth Building built in 1913.

12. This building of more than 55 stories amazed New Yorkers.

13. After the Woolworth Building went up, everyone wanted to build high buildings.

14. The Chrysler Building in 1930 and the Empire State Building in 1931.

15. Just over one year to build the Empire State Building, a record.

16. More than 3,000 workers built it, its design changed 16 times.

17. The tallest building in the world for 41 years.

18. In 1969, Chicago became home to one of the world's tallest buildings.

19. The dark and bulky John Hancock Center.

20. At first people didn't like it, now they love it.

21. It is 1,127 feet high, from the top you can sometimes see across Lake Michigan.

22. There are now skyscrapers all over the world.

23. Many particularly tall ones in China.

24. Do you know which are the world's tallest buildings now?

25. The twin Petronas Towers, built in 1998 in Malaysia.

Read this paragraph from a draft of a personal narrative about a visit to a skyscraper. On a separate sheet of paper, rewrite the paragraph. Correct the fragments and run-ons by adding words or changing punctuation.

Getting to the top of the Sears Tower took only 70 seconds. The elevator was crowded everyone looked a little nervous. Our ears popping all the way up. No time to get really scared, though. When we got to the top, everyone was grinning. The elevator was a lot of fun, it was almost as good as the view.

Direct Quotations

A **direct quotation** is the exact words of a speaker. It is enclosed in quotation marks.

> "I really liked the book you loaned me last week," Marion said.

An **indirect quotation** is a retelling of the speaker's words.

> Marion said that she really enjoyed the book I loaned her last week.

ReView the Rule

- Begin and end a direct quotation with quotation marks.

- If a direct quotation is a sentence, begin it with a capital letter. If the quotation is part of a sentence, do not begin it with a capital letter.

- Place a comma, period, question mark, or exclamation mark that ends a quote inside the quotation marks.

- Set off a phrase identifying the speaker with a comma.

- If a quotation is divided, enclose both parts within quotation marks.

- Do not use quotation marks around an indirect quotation. In an indirect quotation, the speaker's words are often preceded by the word *that*.

Practice

Now let's put what you learned to use. Number your paper 1.–15. Rewrite incorrect sentences to correct any quotations that have punctuation or capitalization errors. If a sentence is correct, write **Correct**.

1. "I really like reading historical fiction, don't you"? Antonio asked his friend Laura.

2. "Yes, said Laura. Some of the stories we read in literature class were really good."

3. "I liked *Number the Stars* by Lois Lowry a lot," she said.

4. Isn't that the story about the family that protects their friends from the Nazis during World War II?" Mai Li asked.

5. Laura answered "Yes, and it certainly made that period of history come alive for me."

6. "There is another story set during World War II that I really like", said Mai Li.

7. "it is called *Journey to Topaz,* and its author is Yoshiko Uchida," she explained.

8. "I know that book," said Antonio. "It's about a Japanese American family that is sent to live in a camp in Utah."

9. Laura wondered "if there were more historical fiction books she could read about World War II."

10. "There probably are", said Mai Li.

11. "People write historical fiction about all different periods, Antonio pointed out."

12. "A few weeks ago," he said, "My sister read a book called *A Long Way to Go* by Zibby O'Neal."

13. "What was that about," Laura wondered?

14. Antonio answered, "It was set in 1917, when American women were trying to get the right to vote."

15. My sister said that she really learned a lot about the struggles women went through.

Read this section from a draft of a historical fiction episode about the opening of the Brooklyn Bridge. On a separate sheet of paper, rewrite the section. Correct any errors with quotations.

> Marisa asked herself whether they would ever get out of the house on time for the ceremony.
>
> "Jason!" she called to her older brother. "we're going to see the bridge opening, not to meet up with your friend Laurinda. Your hair looks good enough"!
>
> Jason answered "Since when did you get to be so clever, little sister? I don't even think Laurinda is interested in the bridge.
>
> "Well, if you're not ready in five minutes, I'm leaving," Marisa said.

The **past tense form of a verb** is used to tell about something that happened in the past. The past tense form does not have a helping verb. The **past participle form of a verb** is used with a helping verb such as *have, has, had, is,* or *was.* Many verbs, called **irregular verbs,** have different forms in the past and past participle.

ReView the Rule

To form the verb of a sentence correctly:

- Do not use the past form of an irregular verb with a helping verb.
- Do not use the past participle form without a helping verb.
- If you are not sure of the correct forms of a verb, check a dictionary.

Practice

Now let's put what you learned to use. Number a separate sheet of paper 1.–25. Read each sentence. If the verb is incorrect, rewrite the verb correctly. If the verb is correct, write **Correct**.

1. English is spoke different ways in different countries.
2. For example, your penpal in Britain may have wrote you a letter about his family's car.
3. He may have chosen to use some words that are unfamiliar to you.
4. Perhaps he said that his family begun to have car problems.
5. He wrote that the boot had been damaged in an accident.
6. He also mentioned that they had recently ran out of petrol and had to pull over onto the verge.
7. Would you have knew which part of the car was the boot?
8. Would you know that they could not go far without petrol, or gas?
9. Would you have understand that the verge of a road is what we call the shoulder?

10. You probably would have saw some unusual spellings as well.

11. If he said that the car's tyres were wore out, you probably would have figured out that those were "tires."

12. But suppose he said that they had drove by a gaol.

13. Your friend would not have meant "goal."

14. What he actually done was to use the British spelling for "jail."

15. In one short letter, your friend would have gave you a real education about British English.

16. If you had gone to Canada recently, you would have found that people there use some British words.

17. Some Canadians might say that a man wore braces rather than suspenders.

18. Some might say that they et porridge rather than oatmeal.

19. You would have ran into these same word choices in England.

20. In many ways, English in Canada and the United States is the same.

21. This is to be expected in countries that have grew up as neighbors.

22. One type of language that has become different in many English-speaking countries is slang.

23. For instance, though both begun from the same language, Jamaican slang and Irish slang are not much alike.

24. Neighbors of ours done some traveling in Australia.

25. I would have went with them if I could, just to hear the funny slang!

Read this paragraph from a draft of an e-mail about Australian slang. On a separate sheet of paper, rewrite the paragraph. Correct the errors with past and past participle verb forms.

Please help me out. A penpal in Australia has just wrote to me, but there are a lot of expressions in his letter that I don't understand. For instance, he said he had went swimming one day last week in the arvo. Does that mean something that he drove around in? While at the beach, he seen something that was very grouse. Does this mean good or bad?

The pronouns *I, we, you, he, she, it,* and *they* are **subject pronouns**.

The pronouns *me, us, you, him, her, it,* and *them* are **object pronouns**.

The pronouns *my, mine, our, ours, your, yours, his, her, hers, its, their,* and *theirs* are **possessive pronouns**.

A pronoun should have a clear **antecedent,** or noun that it refers to.

Review the Rule

- Use subject pronouns as subjects of sentences.
- Use object pronouns as objects following verbs and as objects of prepositions.
- Use possessive pronouns to show ownership or possession. Do not use an apostrophe in a possessive pronoun.
- Each pronoun must have a clear antecedent.
- Pronouns must agree with their antecedents in number and gender.

Practice

Now let's put what you learned to use. Number your paper 1.–20. Choose the pronoun in parentheses ( ) that correctly completes each sentence. Write the pronoun and then label it as either a subject, an object, or a possessive pronoun.

1. Frankie bragged to Denzel and (I/me) that he could eat the hottest kind of pepper in the world.
2. I told Frankie and (he/him) that I wanted to try that pepper, too.
3. However, none of (we/us) were sure what the hottest pepper is.
4. (It/They) probably would be a habanero pepper or its relative, Scotch bonnet.
5. "I think (your/you're) brother tried a habanero once," Denzel said to me.
6. When (my/our) brother came home, I asked him to tell my friends more about peppers.

7. He said that habaneros and Scotch bonnets are grown in Caribbean countries and that we could taste (it/them) in many hot sauces.

8. Then he asked my friends and (I/me) if we had ever tried Thai peppers.

9. (Him/He) and his girlfriend Robin had once eaten them in a soup at a Thai restaurant.

10. These peppers are very tiny, so neither (he nor she/him nor her) noticed them in the soup.

11. All of a sudden (her/their) eyes began watering, and they started to choke.

12. Robin said it was a good lesson about peppers for my brother and (she/her).

13. My brother knew that my friends and (I/me) wanted to try some really hot peppers.

14. He brought (them and me/they and I) some samples from a store in town.

15. The first thing he offered to Frankie and (we/us) was varieties of bird peppers.

16. There were two varieties of bird peppers to sample, and (it/they) seemed very hot.

17. One ounce of the one called Tepin was supposed to be enough to spread (it's/its) heat through 300 gallons of salsa.

18. Frankie began to get very red after (his/their) first taste of Tepin.

19. My brother said that Denzel and (I/me) shouldn't laugh at him.

20. He said that at least (he/him) and Frankie had some guts.

Read this section from a draft of a summary of an article on peppers. On a separate sheet of paper, rewrite the section. Correct any errors with pronouns.

Chile peppers come from many areas of our world, and its popularity with Americans is growing. For Mexicans and we, a favorite use of chile peppers is in salsa. Peppers turn up in other food dishes as well. Their color usually changes when it is drying, often turning red. Sizes range from quite large to very small.

Adjectives, Adverbs

An **adjective** is a word that describes a noun or pronoun. An adjective tells which one, what kind, or how many. It usually comes before the word it describes. It may also follow a linking verb such as *is, feels, seems, sounds, becomes, looks,* or *appears.* An adjective may have a comparative form, formed with the ending *–er* or with *more,* and a superlative form, formed with the ending *–est* or with *most.*

An **adverb** is a word that describes a verb, an adjective, or another adverb. An adverb tells how, when, where, or to what extent. Some adverbs end in *–ly,* but many common ones do not. An adverb may have a comparative form, usually formed with *more,* and a superlative form, usually formed with *most.*

ReView the Rule

- Use an adverb to describe an action verb.
- Use an adjective after a linking verb, to modify the subject.
- Use comparative adjectives and adverbs to compare two things.
- Use superlative adjectives and adverbs to compare more than two things.
- Do not use *–er* and *more,* or *–est* and *most,* together.

Practice

Now let's put what you learned to use. Number your paper 1.–15. Rewrite the sentences that contain errors with adjectives and adverbs. Correct the errors. If a sentence is correct, write **Correct.** Label the comparative and superlative adjectives and adverbs.

1. Being the first person to reach the North or the South Pole was the great goal of many explorers.
2. Of the two poles, the North Pole was reached soonest.
3. Robert Peary, an American explorer, made his earlier of six tries in 1893.
4. His first several attempts to reach the North Pole did not go good.
5. On the first trip, Peary's sled dogs quickly became sickly or froze to death.

6. On his 1895 trip, Peary went a greater distance than he had before, but still did not reach the Pole.

7. In 1902 Peary's team reached 84°16' north, the closer latitude to the Pole that any American had achieved.

8. Even to an experienced explorer like Peary, the unstable Arctic ice appeared extremely treacherously.

9. Peary finally accomplished his goal in 1909, when he reached the Pole safe.

10. The South Pole was reached only a few years more later than the North Pole.

11. Of the two, the South Pole was the most challenging to reach.

12. Ernest Shackleton went farther south than any explorer before him, but he did not reach the Pole.

13. He was trying to figure out the quicker route of all.

14. The first person to make it to the Pole successful was Roald Amundsen, in 1911.

15. He got to the Pole one month sooner than Robert Scott.

Read this paragraph from a draft of a descriptive essay about the work of another Antarctic explorer. On a separate sheet of paper, rewrite the paragraph. Correct the errors with adjectives and adverbs.

Richard Byrd, the earlier aviator ever to fly to the South Pole, built a cow barn at his base in Little America. In 1933 he transported three cows there, a plan that sounded foolishly to some of his associates. The supplies brought in for the cows were substantial, including two years' worth of food. One cow died, but the others did good. The members of Byrd's party had fresh milk daily.

> **Singular subjects** name only one thing. They can be singular nouns or the pronouns *I, he, she,* and *it*. Singular subjects must be used with singular verbs. Singular verbs usually end in *–s* or *–es*.
>
> **Plural subjects** name more than one thing. They can be plural nouns or the pronouns *we* and *they*. Plural subjects, as well as the pronoun *you*, must be used with plural verbs.
>
> **Compound subjects** joined with *and* are generally plural. Compound subjects joined with *or* or *nor* are sometimes singular, sometimes plural.

ReView the Rule

- Use singular subjects with singular verbs. Use plural subjects, as well as the pronoun *you*, with plural verbs.

- Compound subjects joined with *and* are nearly always plural. In compound subjects joined with *or* or *nor*, the verb agrees with the last item in the subject.

- Be sure that the verb agrees with the subject and not with the object of a preposition that comes before the verb.

- To make sure the subject and verb agree in a question, reword the sentence in subject-verb order.

Practice

Now let's use what you've learned. Number your paper from 1.–15. Choose the verb in parentheses ( ) that correctly completes each sentence. Write the verb and the subject of each sentence. If the subject and verb are singular, write **S**; if they are plural, write **P**.

1. An aurora borealis (is/are) not the only unusual light phenomenon in the night sky.

2. The region above storm clouds also (contain/contains) remarkable lights.

3. Sprites, elves, and blue jets (is/are) the names given to these light forms.

4. (Has/Have) you ever heard of these formations before?

5. The flashes of light given off by a sprite (creates/create) a curtain-like effect above thunderstorm clouds.

6. The reddish color of these lights often (fades/fade) to purple.

7. Huge red blobs or an upward-spreading carrot shape (is/are) another pattern a sprite may work itself into.

8. Blue tendrils, in addition to a basic red shape, often (makes/make) up part of a sprite.

9. (Does/Do) these strange lights sound like anything you have ever seen?

10. Generally, they and their dazzling shows (is/are) hard to pick out with the naked eye.

11. A video recorder used in 1989 by a group of scientists (was/were) the first camera to register evidence of sprites.

12. They (was/were) the earliest light phenomenon to be discovered above storm clouds.

13. Blue jets, with their beams of light ascending directly out of a cloud top, (seems/seem) to be associated with hailstorms.

14. The height of these shooting jets (extends/extend) about 30 miles into the air.

15. Unless you (was/were) in exactly the right place at the right time, you probably would not see them.

Read this section from a draft of an observation report on a thunderstorm. On a separate sheet of paper, rewrite the section. Correct any errors with subject-verb agreement.

The huge clouds from the storm blows in quickly. Rumbles of thunder, soft at first but getting louder, begin to echo in the air. A few drops of rain fall, then a few more. The sounds of the thunder gets louder as the rain gets heavier. Suddenly bright flashes of lightning cut through the sky. Thunder and lightning hits at almost the exact second in a huge, frightening blast. We quickly decides that the safest place to be is the basement.

Appositives

An **appositive** is a phrase that identifies a noun. It follows the noun and explains it or gives more information about it. Appositive phrases may be short or fairly long. Usually they are from two or three words to ten or fifteen words.

ReView the Rule

An appositive that is not vital to the meaning of a sentence is set off with commas.

A comma follows the noun that the appositive identifies.

> We volunteer one day each month at The Shelter, **a local nonprofit organization**.

If the appositive comes in the middle of a sentence, a comma follows the last word in the appositive.

> Volunteers, **people who work for no money,** are important to nonprofit organizations.

Practice

Now let's put what you learned to use. Number your paper 1.–15. Rewrite each sentence and correct the punctuation of the appositive.

1. Nonprofit organizations groups that work for a cause without expecting to make a profit can do a lot of good.

2. There are more than one million "recognized" organizations groups with official names and regular employees in the United States alone.

3. Some of these nonprofit organizations work on social issues problems that affect many people across society.

4. Others are involved in medical research cures for cancer or birth defects or in improving care for the mentally ill.

5. Free legal representation a real issue for poor people unjustly accused of crimes is the focus of some groups.

6. A nonprofit that influences many people's lives is public television a source of some excellent programs.

7. The Red Cross a huge nonprofit group that works in many countries often steps in to provide relief for disaster victims.

8. Environmental protection a cause popular with many Americans is the focus of several nonprofit organizations.

9. How do nonprofit groups providers of so many useful services actually work?

10. It is important to understand that "nonprofit" does not necessarily mean free no money involved.

11. Groups must have staffs people to plan and administer programs or else they cannot function.

12. If those staff members are actual employees, they must receive compensation salaries on which to support themselves and their families.

13. To raise the money they need, some nonprofits use direct-mail campaigns requests for donations sent to individuals through the mail.

14. A nonprofit's goal is not to make money, though; it is to provide service help for a worthy cause.

15. For example, the TV-Turnoff Network a group promoting alternatives to watching television does not expect to get rich at their work.

Read this paragraph from a draft of a problem-solution editorial about helping a local nonprofit organization. On a separate sheet of paper, rewrite the paragraph. Correct the errors with appositives by adding commas where they are needed.

Help the Children a nonprofit organization based right here in Novustown needs volunteers between the ages of 14 and 17. The group a provider of baby-sitting care for poor families will work with volunteers to get them to and from children's homes. The group's offices are on Plymouth Courtway a paved alley behind Main Street.

A **business letter** has the following parts: the heading, the inside address, the salutation, the body, the closing, and the signature.

- The **heading** contains the sender's address and the date.

- The **inside address** gives the name and/or title and address of the person to whom the letter is written.

- These parts, together with the **salutation** and **closing,** follow certain capitalization and punctuation rules.

ReView the Rule

- Use commas in the heading only between the city and state, and between the date and the year.

- If the receiver's name is not known, use only that person's title in the inside address.

- Capitalize all words in the heading and all important words in the inside address.

- Capitalize all important words in the greeting, including the person's title, and end the greeting with a colon.

- Capitalize the first word of the closing, and end the closing with a comma.

Negative words are words like *no, not, nothing, nobody, never, nowhere, neither, none,* and the contraction *n't. Hardly, barely, scarcely,* and *without* are also considered to be negative words. Using two negative words together creates the error called a **double negative**.

ReView the Rule

- Do not use more than one negative word to express a negative idea.

Practice

Now let's put what you learned to use. Number your paper 1.–15. If an item contains a letter-form error or a double negative, rewrite it correctly. If an item is correct, write **Correct**.

(1) 522 N. Merrill Avenue,

(2) Tulsa, OK 74137

(3) January 7 20--

(4) Director of recreation

(5) Pleasant Park District Headquarters

(6) 33 w. Hargrove Street

(7) Tulsa, OK, 74137

(8) dear Sir or Madam:

(9) I haven't never received the brochure about winter sports that I ordered four weeks ago. (10) The order form said to contact your office if I had not received it by January 1. (11) Please don't forget to send me a brochure. (12) I really need it as soon as possible. (13) My little brother can't hardly wait to begin taking ice-skating lessons.

(14) Yours Truly,

(15) Carole Anne Henderson

Apply

Read this section from a draft of a persuasive letter. On a separate sheet of paper, rewrite the section. Correct any letter-form errors and double negatives.

In conclusion, lost valuables such as family jewelry can't never be replaced. Your bank will hardly want to take the blame if something else goes wrong. Please do something about the problem quickly. There isn't no time like the present to act decisively.

Yours Very Truly,

Conventions & Skills — Apostrophes

Apostrophes are used to form possessive nouns. They are also used in contractions to show that a letter or letters have been left out.

ReView the Rule

- Singular nouns and plural nouns that don't end in *s* form the possessive by adding *'s*.
- Plural nouns ending in *s* form the possessive by adding an apostrophe.
- An apostrophe replaces the missing letter or letters in a contraction.

Practice

Now let's put what you learned to use. Number your paper 1.–25. Read the sentences below. If a word in a sentence is missing an apostrophe or contains an inappropriately used apostrophe, write the word correctly. If a sentence is correct, write **Correct**.

1. Its difficult to predict who will suffer from high altitude sickness.
2. Some people get it, and some people don't.
3. What exactly is high altitude sickness?
4. As altitude increases, the airs oxygen level decreases.
5. A persons body has to adjust to working with less oxygen.
6. For most people, it takes one to three day's for their body to adjust, or acclimate, to higher altitudes.
7. Going higher before your bodys ready is like asking for trouble.
8. If your body isnt acclimated, serious illness can result.
9. There are rules you can follow to help prevent high altitude sickness.
10. Whenever possible, don't fly or drive to extremely high altitudes.
11. If you must fly or drive to a high altitude, give your body at least 24 hour's to acclimate before you engage in any physical activities there.

12. When youre already in a high altitude, don't increase your altitude more than 1000 feet each day.

13. Once you've reached an extra 3000 feet, give your body a day to re-acclimate.

14. Drink lot's of water to keep your body hydrated.

15. Don't work or play too hard. Light exercise is good, but too much or too little can be harmful.

16. Eat foods with lots of carbohydrates—breads, rice, oatmeal, fruits, and vegetables—when youre at high altitudes.

17. If you notice any symptoms of high altitude sickness, don't go any higher until the symptoms go down.

18. If your symptom's increase, move to a lower altitude.

19. If symptoms persist or continue to get worse, get to a hospital or doctor's office as soon as possible.

20. Remember that people's bodies acclimate at different rates.

21. Give all your groups members enough time to get used to a high altitude.

22. Even mountain climbers know they shouldnt go too far too fast.

23. If you think you have high altitude sickness, remember these two important mountain climbers rules.

24. Dont go up until symptoms go down.

25. If symptoms increase, go down, down, down!

Read this section from a draft of a cause-and-effect essay. On a separate sheet of paper, rewrite the section. Correct any errors with apostrophes.

An invention called the Gamow (pronounced ga' mäf) Bag is used to treat high altitude sickness in the field. Its basically a large bag with a pump. A person gets in the bag and the bag is inflated. The pump fill's the bag with air, increasing the oxygen level inside. The bag starts to work within minutes. After an hour or two, the persons body chemistry is almost normal. The Gamow Bags usefulness is unquestionable.

Proper nouns name particular persons, places, and things. **Initials** and **abbreviations** sometimes stand for or are part of proper nouns. **Proper adjectives** are adjectives that are formed from proper nouns.

ReView the Rule

- Capitalize proper nouns and proper adjectives.
- Capitalize initials and follow them with periods.
- Capitalize abbreviations that are parts of names and follow them with periods.

Practice

Now let's put what you learned to use. Number your paper 1.–20. Copy each item with a capitalization or punctuation error and write it correctly. If an item is correct, write **Correct**.

1. According to several American studies, many foods can help prevent disease.

2. Dr Frieda Nannigan, who works at New york University, has done a number of such studies.

3. She was assisted by Louis Franz, jr. and other scientists.

4. One of her research papers was called "Your Health depends on What You Eat."

5. Studies have been done by European and canadian researchers as well.

6. A Dutch study showed that eating apples might prevent heart attacks.

7. Fred T Hotchkins performed a similar study.

8. He worked with elderly men in california.

9. The name of his study was "the Surprising Effects of Apples."

10. Scientists at the University of western Ontario have done research on oranges and certain kinds of cancer.

11. A study in india has also looked for connections between foods and cancer.

12. The Indian researchers were specifically looking into how eating onions might lower incidences of lung cancer.

13. In 2001, Dr. Christiaan Barnard published a book called <u>50 Ways to a healthy Heart</u>.

14. This famous South african doctor talked about eating fruit, vegetables, and fish.

15. Research on food and health will undoubtedly continue at Universities all over the world.

16. Forrester, Susan, Jack T. Brown, and Martin Feingold. <u>Appreciating Mrs Bloom's Chicken Soup</u>. Dorchester: Decibel Company, 1997.

17. "Nature's Medicine Chest." <u>Maclean's</u> 27 october 1997: 53

18. Smith, Anne. "More Veggies, Please." <u>newsweek</u> Fall/Winter 2001: 43.

19. "What Fruits and Vegetables can Do for You." Natural Health. 4 December 2001 <http://naturalhealth.com/vegetables>.

20. Xanther, t. Price. <u>Many Ways to Better Health</u>. Arlington: Health Press of America, 1996.

Read this paragraph from a research report. On a separate sheet of paper, rewrite the paragraph. Correct the errors with proper nouns and adjectives, initials, and abbreviations.

Some people have been studying the diet of Asian, Australian, and south American men. One of these researchers, Fr. John Waters, is a Catholic priest. In august of 2000 he published a long report summarizing his research. His article, which was published in <u>Gladstone's Biweekly</u>, is entitled "do Some Men's Diets Add Years to Their lives?"

Proofreading Checklist

☑ Do all the sentences have a subject and verb?

☑ Do the subjects and verbs agree?

☑ Does each sentence begin with a capital letter and end with the correct punctuation?

☑ Have sentences been joined with a comma and a joining word or with a semicolon?

☑ Have commas been used correctly?

☑ Have double negatives been avoided?

☑ Have adjectives and adverbs been used correctly?

☑ Do all proper nouns begin with a capital letter?

☑ Have the correct subject and object pronouns been used?

☑ Have the possessive forms of nouns been formed correctly?

☑ Are all words spelled correctly?

Number your paper 1.–25. Check the sentences below for errors in grammar, capitalization, punctuation, and spelling. If a sentence is correct, write **Correct**. If a sentence has an error, rewrite it correctly. A sentence may have more than one error. Use the checklist above to help you.

1. Veterinarians, or vets as they are often called, is not just pet doctors.

2. Vets treat diseases but they also work to prevent disease.

3. Children in a city or town may think a vet is a pet docter.

4. Farmers and their families, who depend on their livestock.

5. A farmers cattle pigs, and sheep provide his income.

6. An epidemic could put a farmer out of busines

7. Vets inspect meat very careful before it is used as food.

8. Zoos employs vets to look after there exotic animals.

9. Vets can choose among many specialties or they can decide to do research and teach.

10. Colleges offering a degree in veterinary medicine should be approved by the american veterinary medical association.

11. Jerry and me are thinking about a career in veterinary medicine.

12. We learned about taking care of our pets from Dr. Lamb.

13. Although I take good care of my dog.

14. Doctor johnson studied for six years to become a vet.

15. She teached me what and when to feed my kittens.

16. If frightened, even the nicer pet can became hostile.

17. Dogs and cats is still the most popular pets.

18. Certain breeds of dogs are recognized by the american kennel club.

19. Were cats held in high regard by ancient Egyptians.

20. Rabbits are also popular pets, and it can be taught simple tricks.

21. Rabbits eat hay clover cabbage, and, of course, carrots.

22. My vet told me that a rabbits teeth never stop growing.

23. She suggests giving a pet rabbit a thick twig, this gives it something to gnaw on.

24. Baby chicks or ducks do not make no good pets.

25. Babys are cute but they are often neglected after they grow up.

Copy the following paragraph. Correct any errors.

A pet rabbit need special care. Never pick up a rabbit by it's ears. Baby bunnies should be handled very little but with good care it will grow up to be very loving pets. Rabbits need a house or shelter. A cardboard box with a hole cut in one side. Don't never put the shelter in a sunny place. Cover the floor of the cage with shavings sawdust or hay and always keep it dry.

Writer's Handbook

The Writer's Handbook is designed to give you more help as well as some great hints for making your writing the best it can be. It uses the Gather, Organize, Write, Elaborate, Clarify, and Proofread categories you have become familiar with during the course of this book. Use the Writer's Handbook any time you have more questions or just need a little extra help.

Table of Contents

Research

Research is an important part of writing. When you research, it's important to use good sources.

A **source** is anything or anyone with information. **Primary sources** include books or people that are closest to the information. **Secondary sources** are books or people who use other books or people to get information. Primary and secondary sources fit into three categories—**printed, electronic,** and **personal.**

- **Printed sources** include books, magazines, newspapers, letters, journals and diaries, and reference materials such as encyclopedias and dictionaries.
- **Electronic sources** include the Internet, television, radio, and videos.
- **Personal sources** include people you interview or observe and your own experiences and memories.

When doing research, keep these points in mind:

- When you use sources, be sure they are **credible** ones that can be trusted to have accurate information. Generally, books, magazines, and reference materials can be considered credible sources.
- Use caution when using Web sites, movies, and television as sources. Check several Web sites and some printed sources on the same topic to be sure you are getting "just the facts." Make sure you have an adult—a teacher or parent—help you as you do research on the Internet.
- Movies and television offer a lot of information, but it is often difficult to tell if the information is fact, fiction, or someone's opinion. Again, double check with other sources and with an adult to be sure you are getting accurate information.

	Printed	Electronic	Personal
Sources	Books, Magazines, Newspapers, Reference Materials, Letters, Journals/Diaries	The Internet, Television, Radio, Videos	Self, Other People
Where to Find Them	Library, Home, School, Bookstores, Discount Department Stores	The Internet, Television, Radio, Stores, Library	**Home:** Parents, Siblings, Grandparents **School:** Teachers, Principals, Librarians, Friends, Other Family Members, People in the Community
How to Use Them	Use headings to find useful information. Read. Take notes.	Read Web sites. Watch or listen to the news. Take notes as you are reading, watching, and listening.	Interview people. Ask questions. Take notes.
How to Cite Them (Use punctuation and capitalization as shown.)	**Books:** Author's Last Name, First Name. Book Title. City: Publishing Company, year. **Magazine Articles:** Author's Last Name, First Name. "Title of Article." Title of Magazine, volume number (if there is one), date, month, or season, and year of publication: page number. (If the article is longer than one page, state the first page and the last page of the article with a dash between them.) **Encyclopedias/Dictionaries:** Title of Encyclopedia or Dictionary, edition number (ed. __), s.v. "item." (If you looked up Olympic Games, it would be s.v. "Olympic Games.") **Letters/Diaries/Journals:** Mention them in the text as you are writing.	**Internet:** State the Web address of the Web sites you used. Most Web addresses will begin with http:// and end with .com, .net, .org, or .edu. **Films/Videos:** Title of Film or Video. City where the production company is located: Production Company Name, year. **Television/Radio:** Mention them in the text as you are writing.	Personal sources should be mentioned in the text as you are writing. When interviewing, you can quote the person by enclosing his or her exact words in quotation marks. You can also use phrases such as "according to" to give credit to your source. To give credit to personal sources other than people you interview, simply state where you found the information.

Getting Ideas for Writing

Brainstorming

Brainstorming is a great way to generate lots of ideas in a short amount of time. You can brainstorm alone or with a group of people. All you have to do is say or think one word, and you're off! Here's how it works:

One person starts by saying a word. The rest of the group can now take turns saying words or phrases that come to mind. As the process continues, you or someone else in the group will probably say something that will become the topic for your writing.

Journaling

A journal is similar to a diary. Both are used to write down personal thoughts. However, diaries are usually used to record daily events and feelings. Journals are generally used to record thoughts, impressions, and responses to events. A journal is a great way to generate ideas for writing.

Freewriting

Freewriting is a very unusual method of writing because it has no form. The idea behind freewriting is to write down everything that comes to mind during a specific period of time. Just get out a piece of paper and a pen or pencil, or sit down in front of a computer. For the next few minutes, jot down everything your mind comes up with.

When time is up, stop writing and look at what you've got. Read it over a couple of times. You'll be amazed at what you might find. Some of the best ideas for writing show up in the middle of freewriting.

Daydreaming

Try this. When you have some free time at home, get a mug of something good to drink (hot chocolate works great on a cold day). Now find a comfortable spot and—are you ready for this?—don't do anything! At least, don't do anything specific. Daydreaming means letting your mind wander wherever it wants to. Stare out the window. Watch the goldfish in your fish tank. Listen to the rain. Smell dinner cooking in the kitchen. Think about what you'll be when you're an adult. Something will probably come to mind that will make a great topic for writing.

Reading

Sometimes the easiest way to get ideas for writing is to read. Make use of your library. Talk to your school librarian or go to the public library and ask for help at the information desk. As you read, you will spot things that interest you. Write down those things. When you are finished reading, look at the notes you took. Somewhere in your notes you may have a great idea for writing.

TV/Movies

Great ideas for writing may be as close as your television or movie theater. There are cable channels that run programs specifically about science, technology, history, animals, cooking, music, sports, and just about any other topic you can think of. Public television also has great documentaries and programs about interesting and unusual topics. Movies can also be good for generating ideas for writing—especially movies that deal with specific topics. Just as you should use caution when using television and movies as sources when you write, be cautious in using them to generate ideas. Make sure you talk to an adult about appropriate and safe choices in movies and television programs.

Interviewing

An interview is the process of asking questions of another person and listening to and recording that person's answers. Interviews make good sources for writing projects, especially if the person you interview is an expert about your topic. Interviews can also be good ways to generate ideas for writing.

Some of the most interesting stories come from people in your community and family. Your parents and grandparents have lived through many events. Sit down with a family member or another trusted adult and ask that person to tell you about a memorable event he or she experienced or an interesting person he or she knew. You'll be amazed at the stories you will hear. Many famous authors say that their stories were inspired by what other people have told them.

As you listen to people's stories, jot down notes. It's safe to say that something the person said during the interview will probably give you a good idea for your own writing project.

Prewriting Organize

Note Taking

As you are doing research for your writing project, you will want to take notes. That way you will have the most important information in small pieces that you can use easily. Here are some things to keep in mind:

- Keep your notes short. You don't have to use complete sentences, as long as you include the important information.

- Make sure your handwriting is legible. If you scribble, you may not be able to read your own notes later.

- Use note cards. That way you can arrange your notes without having to rewrite them. Try using different colors of note cards to help you organize your notes.

- When listening to a speaker and taking notes, don't try to write down what the speaker is saying "word for word." Just make sure you get the important stuff.

- When you are interviewing, however, you will want to get the exact words down on paper. In this case, ask the speaker to repeat what he or she said so you can write the quote. If it's possible, use a tape recorder during the interview, so you can listen to the quote as often as you need to. Just make sure you get the speaker's permission to record the interview.

- It's important to write down the source of your information on your note cards as you are taking notes. That way you can cite or credit your sources easily.

Graphic Organizers

A graphic organizer is a tool that helps writers put information in order before they start a draft. In this book, you have practiced working with lots of graphic organizers. You have worked with 5 W's charts, story maps, order of importance organizers, main-idea tables, webs, observation charts, problem-solution frames, persuasion maps, cause-and-effect chains, time lines, pro-and-con charts, story boards, sequence chains, and outlines. When you do other writing projects, you'll want to continue to use them to help you keep track of information. What kind of graphic organizers you use depends on what kind of writing project you have. Check back with this book to see what kind of graphic organizer works best for different writing projects.

Outlining

There are many ways to organize information. One very useful organizer that you have used is an outline. The outline helps you put your information in the order it will appear in your writing. The outline can be divided into several basic pieces—the introduction, the body, and the conclusion—just like a basic essay. Every letter and number in the outline stands for something in your essay. Words or phrases that are indicated with Roman numerals represent entire chunks of an essay. Words or phrases that are indicated with capital letters represent paragraphs which support a main statement or idea. Words or phrases that are indicated with regular numbers represent specific details. Here's a basic outline.

I. Introduction

gets audience's attention ──────→ A. Lead

moves closer to the main idea ──────→ B. Related statement

states main idea of essay ──────→ C. Transitional statement

> introduce the essay to the audience

II. Body

states main idea of paragraph ──────→ A. First main idea

  1. First supporting detail
  2. Second supporting detail
  3. Third supporting detail

> support, explain, and give more information about main idea of essay

B. Second main idea

  1. First supporting detail
  2. Second supporting detail
  3. Third supporting detail

> same as paragraph A

C. Third main idea

  1. First supporting detail
  2. Second supporting detail
  3. Third supporting detail

> same as paragraphs A and B

III. Conclusion

restates main ideas of body paragraphs ──────→ A. Brief summary of main ideas

begins to wrap up essay ──────→ B. Other related statement

ends the essay ──────→ C. Closing statement

> wrap up essay

Write

Writing Paragraphs

For example, let's say your essay is a persuasive speech designed to get your audience to vote for a specific candidate for class president. You have gathered information about this person and made a persuasion map to put your information in order. Your persuasion map may look something like this:

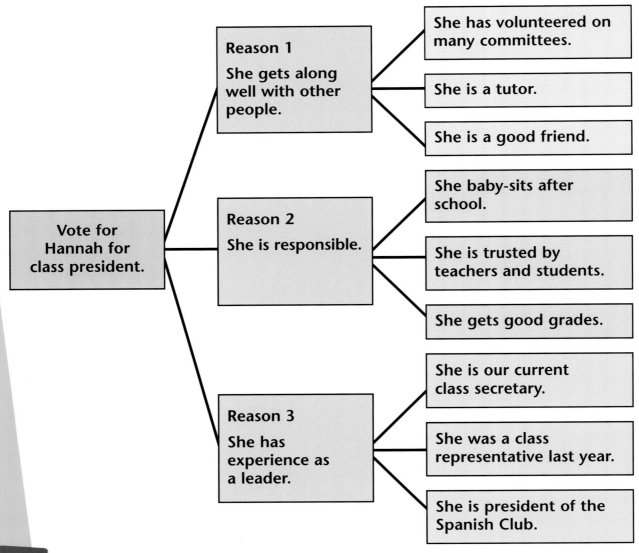

Take your first main point—She gets along well with other people. Write it as a sentence. You might come up with this:

> One excellent reason to vote for Hannah is that she gets along well with other people.

This is now your topic sentence. Now it's time to tell your audience more information about the main idea. Use the details for that main idea to write good persuasive sentences.

> 1. Hannah has demonstrated her ability to work with others by volunteering on many committees, including the dance committee, the fall festival committee, and the book drive committee.
> 2. She works with many people at our school as a tutor, and she is well liked and respected by all of them.
> 3. Hannah is also a good friend who is trusted and liked by many people in our school.

When you combine your topic sentence with these supporting sentences, you have a paragraph.

> One excellent reason to vote for Hannah is that she gets along well with other people. Hannah has demonstrated her ability to work with others by volunteering on many committees, including the dance committee, the fall festival committee, and the book drive committee. She works with many people at our school as a tutor, and she is well liked and respected by all of them. Hannah is also a good friend who is trusted and liked by many people in our school.

Following the same steps for your other two main ideas will give you two more paragraphs. Put these together, and you will have the body of a well-organized persuasive speech. All you need now is an introduction and a conclusion. For tips about writing good introductions and conclusions see "Writing a Five-Paragraph Essay" on page HB 12.

Writing a Five-Paragraph Essay

An essay is a piece of nonfiction writing about one topic. Essays can take many forms. In grades 7 and 8, you practice writing a descriptive essay, a problem-solution essay, a cause-and-effect essay, and a persuasive essay. Essays are made up of three basic parts—the introduction, the body, and the conclusion.

Write the body of your essay first. It doesn't matter that you don't have an introduction yet. It's very difficult to write a good introduction until you have written the body. Imagine trying to introduce a person you don't know to an audience. What would you say? That's kind of what it's like to try writing an introduction first. You don't know your essay yet. Write the body first and then you'll know what to say in your introduction.

Body

The body of your essay is where you explain, describe, prove, and give information about your main idea. Look at your graphic organizer. There's a good chance that you already have the makings of several good paragraphs.

Let's pretend you're writing a descriptive essay of your favorite meal—Thanksgiving dinner. After gathering and organizing your information, you may have four main points in your graphic organizer—how the food looks, how the food tastes, the smells, and the sounds of family. Look at the web on page HB 13.

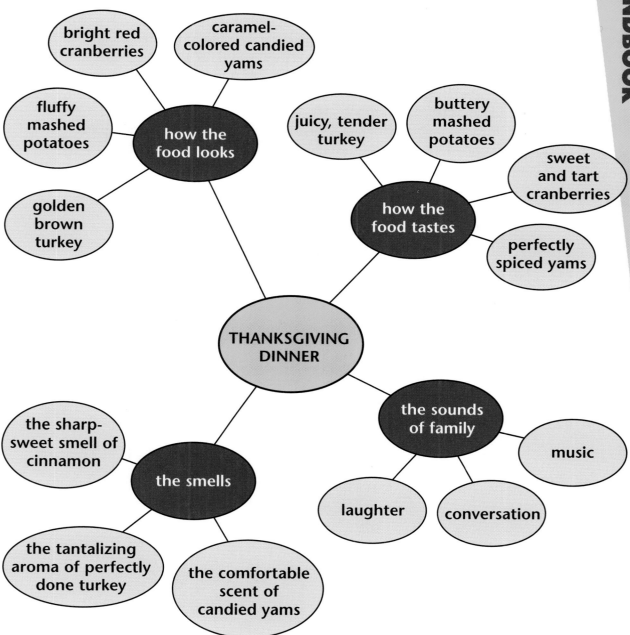

bright red cranberries

caramel-colored candied yams

fluffy mashed potatoes

how the food looks

golden brown turkey

juicy, tender turkey

buttery mashed potatoes

how the food tastes

sweet and tart cranberries

perfectly spiced yams

THANKSGIVING DINNER

the sharp-sweet smell of cinnamon

the smells

the sounds of family

music

laughter

conversation

the tantalizing aroma of perfectly done turkey

the comfortable scent of candied yams

Introduction

The introduction is the first part of the essay that your audience will read or hear. You want it to get their attention and make them interested enough to keep reading or listening. What you don't want to do is give away what's in the essay. If you do, your audience will have no reason to keep reading or listening.

The Upside-Down Pyramid

If your introduction were a graphic organizer, it would look like an upside-down pyramid. Let's write an introduction for our essay about the Thanksgiving dinner.

The first sentence of your introduction should say something true but general about your topic.

One of the most enjoyable experiences in life is a good meal.

This sentence gives some examples of enjoyable experiences. It's still pretty general, but it gets closer to the main idea.

Having a good meal with your family is even more special.

This sentence should be the main idea of your essay.

For the sights, tastes, smells, and sounds, nothing is better than Thanksgiving dinner.

Here's the complete introduction:

One of the most enjoyable experiences in life is a good meal. Having a good meal with your family is even more special. For the sights, tastes, smells, and sounds, nothing is better than Thanksgiving dinner.

Conclusion

The conclusion of an essay does two things. It restates the main idea of the essay, and it wraps up the essay. Restating the main idea is important. You want to make sure your audience remembers what the essay was about. Wrapping things up helps the audience feel that they have read a complete work and that nothing is missing.

The Right-Side-Up Pyramid

If the introduction of your essay looks like an upside-down pyramid, the conclusion looks like a pyramid right-side-up. Here's how:

The first sentence of the conclusion
should restate the main idea.

With gorgeous and delicious food,
wonderful smells, and the sounds of family,
Thanksgiving dinner is one of the best parts of the year.

The next sentence should say
something a little more general but still
stay on the main idea.

It's always great to celebrate important
events with good food and people you love.

The final sentence should wrap things up and finish the essay.
It should be very general.

Everyone celebrates differently, but every celebration is special.

When you put your conclusion together, it will look like this:

With gorgeous and delicious food, wonderful smells, and the sounds of family, Thanksgiving dinner is one of the best parts of the year. It's always great to celebrate important events with good food and people you love. Everyone celebrates differently, but every celebration is special.

Writing Poetry

Poetry is different from other forms of writing. Some poems are written in lines and stanzas and follow a rhyme or rhythm. Some poems are simply words or phrases with no rhyme (free verse). Most poems are full of imagery or word pictures. Whatever form a poem takes, it's one of the most creative forms of writing.

When you start to write a poem, the first thing to do is to pick a subject. It's a good idea to pick a subject that you know something about or a subject that means a lot to you. Next you should try to write down interesting ideas about your subject. You can write down your ideas however you like.

Then it is time to write your first draft. Once again, you can use any form you like to write your poem. Be sure to use plenty of descriptive words, or words that describe sounds, smells, tastes, and how things look and feel. As you begin to write, your poem might already be taking on its own form.

Revising is an important part of all writing, including writing poetry. You'll probably revise your poem many times. You might want to try changing the form of your poem. Once it's written, you may think it would be better stated in rhyme. You may think your poem is better if it doesn't rhyme. Just make sure your poem's message and ideas are clear to your readers.

Once you have written your final version, read it over to yourself. Then read it out loud. You may find more areas to improve.

Revising
Elaborate and Clarify

Thesaurus

When it comes to saying things in different, more interesting ways, the thesaurus is one of the best friends a writer can have.

A thesaurus is a reference book which lists the *synonyms* (words that have the same or similar meaning) of words, and the *antonyms* (words that have the opposite meaning) of words.

Dictionary

One of the most helpful tools for writers is the dictionary. Just think of it! Every word you could possibly need is in there.

Besides the spellings of words, your dictionary contains valuable information, such as the history of words, a guide for pronunciation, foreign words and phrases, the names of historical people, the names of places in the world, and lots of other interesting things. Some dictionaries even contain the Declaration of Independence and the Constitution of the United States!

Web Sites

With the help of an adult, try these Web sites for even more help in building your vocabulary and making your writing richer and clearer.

http://www.writetools.com
This is a one-stop Web site for writers. It contains links to reference materials, almanacs, calendars, historical documents, government resources, grammar and style guides, and all kinds of other tools for writing and editing.

http://www.bartleby.com
This Web site has links to several on-line dictionaries, encyclopedias, thesauri, and many other useful and interesting sources. It also contains links to on-line fiction and nonfiction books. It's like having a library of your own.

Capitalization

Capitalize:

- the first word in a sentence.
- all proper nouns, including people's names and the names of particular places.
- titles of respect.
- family titles used just before people's names and titles of respect that are part of names.
- initials of names.
- place names.
- proper adjectives, adjectives that are made from proper nouns.
- the months of the year and the days of the week.
- important words in the names of organizations.
- important words in the names of holidays.
- the first word in the greeting or closing of a letter.
- the word *I*.
- the first, last, and most important words in a title. Be sure to capitalize all verbs, including *is* and *was*.
- the first word in a direct quotation.

Sentence Structure

The Sentence

A sentence is a group of words that tells a complete thought. A sentence has two parts: a **subject** and a **predicate**.

- The complete subject tells whom or what the sentence is about.
  Joe walked home.

- The complete predicate tells what happened.
  Joe **walked home**.

There are four kinds of sentences: **declarative, interrogative, imperative,** and **exclamatory**.

- A **declarative** sentence makes a statement and ends with a period.
  I just ate lunch**.**

- An **interrogative** sentence asks a question and ends with a question mark.
  Did you eat lunch**?**

- An **imperative** sentence gives a command and usually ends with a period.
  Turn down that loud music**.**

- A firm command can end with an exclamation point.
  Shut the door**!**

- An **exclamatory** sentence expresses strong feelings and ends with an exclamation point.
  That music is too loud!

Subjects

The **subject** of a sentence tells whom or what the sentence is about.

- A sentence can have one subject.
  Joe walked home.

- A sentence can have a **compound subject,** two or more subjects that are joined by a conjunction *(and, or)* and that share the same predicate.
  Joe and **Martha** walked to school.

- Imperative sentences have an unnamed **understood subject,** the person being spoken to. This subject is referred to as "understood *you*."
  Close the window.

- The **complete subject** includes all the words that name and tell about the subject.
  The main road in our city is called Broad Street.

- The **simple subject** is the most important noun or pronoun in the complete subject.
  The main **road** in our city is called Broad Street.

Note: Sometimes the simple subject and the complete subject are the same.
  Joe walked home.

Predicates

The **predicate** of a sentence tells what happened. The **complete predicate** includes a verb and all the words that tell what happened.

- A complete predicate can include an action verb to tell what the subject of the sentence did.
  Joe **walked home**.

- A complete predicate can include a linking verb to tell more about the subject.
  Her dress **is blue**.

- The **simple predicate** is the most important word or words in the complete predicate. The simple predicate is always a verb.
  Joe **walked** home.

- A **compound predicate** is two or more predicates that share the same subject. Compound predicates are often joined by the conjunction *and* or *or*.
  Jessie **climbed** a tree and **read** her book.

- A **predicate** noun follows a linking verb and renames the subject.
  Tom is the **author** of that book.

- A **predicate adjective** follows a linking verb and describes the subject.
  Her dress is **blue**.

Simple, Compound, and Complex Sentences

- A **simple sentence** tells one complete thought.
  Joe walked home.

- A **compound sentence** is made up of two simple sentences (or **independent clauses**) whose ideas are related. The clauses can be joined by a comma and a conjunction *(and, or, but)*.
  The helicopter landed on the field**, and** a crowd gathered around it.

- The two independent clauses in a compound sentence can also be joined by a semicolon.
  The helicopter landed on the field**;** a crowd gathered around it.

- Two clauses in a compound sentence can be separated by a colon when the second clause is a direct result of the first clause.
  The diver knew what to do**:** he told the captain.

- A **complex sentence** is made up of one **independent clause** and at least one **dependent clause**. A **dependent clause** is a group of words that has a subject and a predicate, but it cannot stand on its own.
    Dependent Clause: When the roller coaster topped the first hill
    Independent Clause: I let out a wild scream
    Complex Sentence: When the roller coaster topped the first hill, I let out a wild scream.

- A **compound-complex sentence** includes two or more independent clauses and at least one dependent clause.
    Independent Clauses: Isabel began painting two years ago
        she has been asked to hang a painting at the art exhibit
    Dependent Clause: that is scheduled for next month
    Compound-complex Sentence: Isabel began painting two years ago, and she has been asked to hang a painting at the art exhibit that is scheduled for next month.

- An **adjective clause** is a dependent clause that describes a noun or pronoun. An adjective clause always follows the word it describes and begins with a relative pronoun such as *who, whom, whose, which,* or *that.*
    My brother**, who wanted to come,** could not attend the party.

- An **adverb clause** is a dependent clause that tells more about a verb, an adjective, or an adverb. Adverb clauses tell *where, when, why,* or *how much.* They often begin with a subordinating conjunction such as *after, since, where, than, although, because, if, as, as if, while, when,* or *whenever.*
    When you hit your funny bone, you strike a sensory nerve.

Subject-Verb Agreement

The subject and its verb must agree in number. Be sure that the verb agrees with its subject and not with the object of a preposition that comes before the verb.
    One **part** of speech **is** a noun. (*Part* is singular, so it requires the verb *is.*)
    The **sweatshirts** on the rack **were** on sale. (*Sweatshirts* is a plural, so it requires the verb *were.*)

A compound subject and its verb must agree.

- Compound subjects joined by *and* are plural.
    Jack and Jill carry the bucket. (plural verb)

- If a compound subject is joined by *or,* the verb must agree with the last item in the subject.
    The **boys or Jill carries** the bucket. (singular verb)

There are special rules for agreement with certain kinds of subjects.

- **Titles** of books, movies, magazines, newspapers, stories, and songs are always considered singular, even if they end in *s*.
    The Outsiders **is** my favorite book.

- A **collective noun**, such as *collection, group, team, country, kingdom, family, flock,* and *herd*, names more than one person or object acting as a group. These nouns are usually considered singular.
    Our **country is** quite large.

- Most **indefinite pronouns**, including *everyone, nobody, nothing, everything, something,* and *anything*, are considered singular.
    Anything is possible if you try.

- Some **indefinite pronouns** that clearly refer to more than one, such as *many, most, few,* and *both*, are considered plural.
    Few are going on the trip.

Abbreviations

Abbreviations are shortened forms of words. Many abbreviations begin with a capital letter and end with a period.

Abbreviate:

- words used in addresses.

Street (St.)	Boulevard (Blvd.)	Route (Rt.)
Avenue (Ave.)	Road (Rd.)	

- the names of states when you address envelopes.
    Note: State names are abbreviated as two capital letters, with no periods.

Alabama (AL)	Idaho (ID)	Missouri (MO)	Pennsylvania (PA)
Alaska (AK)	Illinois (IL)	Montana (MT)	Rhode Island (RI)
Arizona (AZ)	Indiana (IN)	Nebraska (NE)	South Carolina (SC)
Arkansas (AR)	Iowa (IA)	Nevada (NV)	South Dakota (SD)
California (CA)	Kansas (KS)	New Hampshire (NH)	Tennessee (TN)
Colorado (CO)	Kentucky (KY)	New Jersey (NJ)	Texas (TX)
Connecticut (CT)	Louisiana (LA)	New Mexico (NM)	Utah (UT)
Delaware (DE)	Maine (ME)	New York (NY)	Vermont (VT)
District of	Maryland (MD)	North Carolina (NC)	Virginia (VA)
Columbia (DC)	Massachusetts (MA)	North Dakota (ND)	Washington (WA)
Florida (FL)	Michigan (MI)	Ohio (OH)	West Virginia (WV)
Georgia (GA)	Minnesota (MN)	Oklahoma (OK)	Wisconsin (WI)
Hawaii (HI)	Mississippi (MS)	Oregon (OR)	Wyoming (WY)

- titles of address and titles of respect. (Dr., Gov.)

- certain words in the names of businesses. (Corp., Inc.)

- days of the week when you take notes.
  Sunday (Sun.)   Tuesday (Tues.)   Thursday (Thurs.)   Saturday (Sat.)
  Monday (Mon.)   Wednesday (Wed.)   Friday (Fri.)

- most months of the year when you take notes.
  January (Jan.)   April (Apr.)   October (Oct.)
  February (Feb.)   August (Aug.)   November (Nov.)
  March (Mar.)   September (Sept.)   December (Dec.)
  (May, June, and July do not have abbreviated forms.)

- directions when you take notes.
  North (N)   East (E)   South (S)   West (W)

Titles

- Underline titles of books, newspapers, TV series, movies, and magazines.
  Note: These titles are written in italics in printed text.
      The New York Times, *The Wind in the Willows*

- Use quotation marks around articles in magazines, short stories, chapters in books, songs, and poems.
      "The Raven"

- Capitalize the first, last, and most important words in titles. Articles, short prepositions, and conjunctions are usually not capitalized. Be sure to capitalize all verbs, including forms of the verb *be (am, is, are, was, were, been)*.

Quotation Marks

- Put **quotation marks** (" ") around the titles of articles, short stories, book chapters, songs, and poems.

- Put quotation marks around a **direct quotation,** or a speaker's exact words.
      Tom said, "I don't want to go."

- Do not put quotation marks around an **indirect quotation,** a person's words retold by another speaker. An indirect quotation is often signaled by *whether* or *that*.
      Tom said that he didn't want to go.

End Marks

Every sentence must end with a **period,** an **exclamation point,** or a **question mark**.

- Use a **period** at the end of a statement (declarative sentence)
    They walked across the bridge**.**
  or a command (imperative sentence).
    Shut the door**.**

- Use an **exclamation point** at the end of a firm command (imperative sentence)
    Stop that!
  or at the end of a sentence that shows great feeling or excitement (exclamatory sentence).
    That pan is hot!

- Use a **question mark** at the end of an asking sentence (interrogative sentence).
    Does eating bread crust make your hair curly?

Apostrophes

An **apostrophe** (') is used to form the possessive of a noun or to join words in a contraction.

- **Possessives** show ownership. To make a singular noun possessive, add *'s*.
    the girl**'s** book

- To form a possessive from a plural noun that ends in *s,* add only an apostrophe.
    the dresse**s'** belts

- Some plural nouns do not end in *s*. To form possessives with these nouns, add *'s*.
    children**'s** laughter

- Use an apostrophe to replace the dropped letters in a **contraction**.
    isn't, can't

Commas, Semicolons, and Colons

Commas in Sentences

Use a **comma**:

- after an introductory word in a sentence.
  No, I don't think so.

- to separate items in a series of three or more items. Put the last comma before *and* or *or*.
  We ate hamburgers, potato salad, and watermelon.

- to separate a noun of direct address from the rest of a sentence.
  Ellen, where have you been?

- to separate an appositive from the rest of the sentence.
  My bicycle, the red one over there, has a flat tire.

- to separate a direct quotation from the rest of a sentence.
  The announcer warned, "Severe storms are approaching our area."

- with the conjunction *and, or,* or *but* when combining independent clauses in a compound sentence.
  He could play soccer, **or** he could run track.

- to separate a dependent clause at the beginning of a sentence from the rest of the sentence.
  When the roller coaster topped the first hill, I let out a wild scream.

Semicolons and Colons in Sentences

- You may use a **semicolon** in place of a comma and a conjunction when combining independent clauses.
  Bicycles used to be much harder to ride; they didn't come with 21 speeds.

- A **colon** can be used when the second clause states a direct result of the first or explains the first.
  The diver knew what to do: he told the captain.

- Use a **colon** to introduce a list or series.
  The art kit included: paint, brushes, crayons, and pastels.

- Use a **colon** after the greeting in a business letter.
  Dear Sir:

- Use a **colon** to separate hours and minutes in an expression of time.
  11:35

- Use a **colon** between the city of publication and the publisher in a bibliographical reference.
  New York: Ballantine Books

Hyphens and Parentheses

Hyphens in Sentences

Use a hyphen:

- to separate the syllables when you break a word at the end of a line.
  sense-less

- to link the parts of some compound words.
  self-esteem, far-fetched

- to link some pairs or groups of words that precede a noun and act as an adjective.
  thirteen-year-old girl

- to link the parts of numbers between twenty-one and ninety-nine.
  thirty-two, forty-five

Parentheses in Sentences

Use **parentheses**:

- to set off an explanation.
  The Rock of Gibraltar is 1,398 feet **(426 meters)** tall.

- to set off an example.
  Speleologists **(scientists who study caves)** are fascinated by Gorham Cave.

Parts of Speech

Nouns

- A **common noun** names any person, place, thing, or idea.
  dog   boy   governor

- A **proper noun** names a certain person, place, thing, or idea. Proper nouns begin with a capital letter. A proper noun that is made up of two or more words is considered one noun.
  Rover   James   Governor Taft

- A **collective noun** names a group of people or things that act as one unit.
  class   herd   group

Plural Nouns

- A singular noun names one person, place, thing, or idea.
  dog   girl   wish

- A plural noun names more than one person, place, thing, or idea. To make most singular nouns plural, add *-s*.
  dog/dogs   girl/girls

- For nouns ending in *sh, ch, x,* or *z,* add *-es* to make the word plural.
  wish/wishes   fox/foxes

- For nouns ending in a consonant and *y,* change the *y* to *i* and add *-es*.
  family/families   story/stories

- For some nouns that end in *f* or *fe,* replace *f* or *fe* with *ves* to make the noun plural.
  knife/knives   shelf/shelves

- Some words change spelling when the plural is formed.
  man/men   child/children

- Some words have the same singular and plural form.
  deer/deer   moose/moose

Possessive Nouns

A possessive shows ownership.

- To make a singular noun possessive, add an apostrophe and *-s*.
  girl/girl's   chair/chair's

- When a singular noun ends in *s,* add an apostrophe and *-s*.
  dress/dress's   glass/glass's

- To make a plural noun that ends in *s* possessive, add an apostrophe.
  wish/wishes'   family/families'

- When a plural noun does not end in *s,* add an apostrophe and *-s* to show possession.
  children/children's   women/women's

Verbs

Action Verb

- An **action verb** shows action.
  Joe **walked** home. The girls **jumped** rope.

Linking Verb

- A **linking verb** does not show action. It connects the subject of a sentence to a word or words in the predicate that tell about the subject. Linking verbs include *am, is, are, was, been,* and *were. Seem, appear,* and *become* can be used as linking verbs, too.
  The dress **is** blue. The apples **seem** ripe.

- Some verbs, such as *appear, look, smell, feel, grow,* and *taste,* can be either action verbs or linking verbs, depending on how they are used. You can test whether a verb is a linking verb by substituting a form of the verb *be* (*am, is, are, was,* or *were*) in its place. If the form of *be* makes sense, the verb is a linking verb.

Main Verbs and Auxiliary Verbs

- A **main verb** is the most important verb in a sentence. An **auxiliary verb,** or **helping verb,** comes before the main verb to help it show action. Auxiliary verbs such as *had, are,* and *will* indicate the tense of the main verb. Others, such as *could, might,* and *may,* show how likely it is that something will happen.
  We **had wanted** to go to the zoo. John **is coming** with us.

The Principal Parts of a Verb

Each verb has three principal parts: its **present form,** its **past form,** and its **past participle** form.

- Most verbs add *-ed* to the present form to create both the past form and the past participle form. These verbs are called **regular verbs.**
  climb/climbed   walk/walked   drop/dropped

- **Irregular verbs** form their past and past participle forms in other ways. The chart below shows the principal parts of several common irregular verbs:

Present	Past	Past Participle
(be) is	was	been
blow	blew	blown
bring	brought	brought
drive	drove	driven
eat	ate	eaten
fly	flew	flown
give	gave	given
go	went	gone
grow	grew	grown
hide	hid	hidden
know	knew	known
lay	laid	laid
lie	lay	lain
ring	rang	rung
say	said	said
see	saw	seen
shake	shook	shaken
sing	sang	sung
swim	swam	swum
take	took	taken
think	thought	thought
throw	threw	thrown
write	wrote	written

- Almost all verbs add *-ing* to the present form to create the **present participle** form.

    sing/singing   talk/talking

Verb Tense

Verb tense places an action in time.

- The **present tense** is used to show that something happens regularly or is true now.
  - Add *-s* to most verbs to show present tense when the subject is *he, she, it,* or a singular noun.

    He **walks** to the park.
  - Add *-es* to verbs ending in *s, ch, sh, x,* or *z*.

    She **wishes** on a star.
  - Do not add *-s* or *-es* if the subject is a plural noun or *I, you, we,* or *they*.

    I want to go to the park.
  - Change *y* to *i* and add *-es* to form some present tense verbs.

    Joe **hurries** to the park.

- The **past tense** shows past action. Add -*ed* to most verbs to form the past tense.

  Joe **walked** home.

- Verbs that do not add -*ed* are called *irregular verbs*.

  Joe **ran** home.

- The **future tense** shows future action. Use the verb *will* to form the future tense.

  Joe **will walk** home tomorrow.

- The **present perfect tense** shows action that began in the past and may still be happening. To form the present perfect tense, add the helping verb *has* or *have* to the past participle of a verb.

  Joe **has walked** home before.

- The **past perfect tense** shows action that was completed by a certain time in the past. To form the past perfect tense, add the helping verb *had* to the past participle of a verb.

  Joe **had walked** to the store.

- The **future perfect tense** shows action that will be complete by a certain time in the future. To form the future perfect tense, add the helping verbs *will have* to the past participle form of a verb.

  Joe **will have walked** home twice this week.

- The **progressive tenses** show continuing action. To form the **present progressive** tense, add *am, is,* or *are* to the *present participle* of a verb (usually the present form + -*ing*).

  Joe **is walking** home.

To form the **past progressive** tense, add *was* or *were* to the present participle.

  Joe **was walking** home.

To form the **future progressive** tense, add *will be* to the present participle.

  Joe **will be walking** home tomorrow.

Verbals

Sometimes a verb does not act as a predicate. **Verbals** are forms of verbs that play other roles in sentences.

- One type of verbal, a **participle,** acts as an adjective. A participle may be the present participle or the past participle form of a verb.

    George heard the bell **ringing**.

    A **participial phrase** is made up of a participle and other words that complete its meaning.

    Matt saw a skunk **waddling through the bushes**.

Pronouns

A **pronoun** can replace a noun.

Personal Pronouns

Personal pronouns include *I, me, you, we, us, he, she, it, they,* and *them*. Personal pronouns can be used to stand for the person speaking, the person spoken to, or the person spoken about.

- **First person pronouns** refer to the speaker *(I, me)* or include the speaker *(we, us)*.

    I love to read. **We** went to the park.

- **Second person pronouns** refer to the person or people being spoken to (you).

    You didn't eat lunch.

- **Third person pronouns** refer to the person, people, or thing(s) being spoken about *(he, him, she, her, it, they, them)*.

    They went to the park. **She** enjoys reading to **him**.

Pronoun Antecedents

An **antecedent** is the word or phrase a pronoun refers to. The antecedent always includes a noun.

- A pronoun must agree with its antecedent. An antecedent and a pronoun agree when they have the same **number** (singular or plural) and **gender** (male or female).

    Joyce is in **her** bedroom.

Possessive Pronouns

Possessive pronouns show ownership.

- The possessive pronouns *my, your, his, her, its, their,* and *our* replace possessive nouns.
  My house is white. **Our** dog loves to fetch.

- The possessive pronouns *mine, ours, yours, hers, his, its,* and *theirs* replace both a possessive noun and the noun that is possessed.
  This book is **mine**. Those coats are **theirs**.

- *Whose* is the possessive form of the relative pronoun *who*. It is also used as the possessive form of the relative pronoun *which*.
  Whose book is this?

Adjectives

An **adjective** is a word that tells more about a noun or a pronoun.

- Some adjectives tell what kind.
  The **bright** sunlight hurt my eyes.

- Some adjectives tell how many.
  Two men did the job.

- A **predicate adjective** follows a linking verb and describes the subject.
  The dress is **blue**.

- *A, an,* and *the* are special kinds of adjectives called **articles**. Use *a* and *an* to refer to any person, place, thing, or idea. Use *the* to refer to a specific person, place, thing, or idea. Use *a* before a singular noun that begins with a consonant sound. Use *an* before a singular noun that begins with a vowel sound.
  an apple, **a** dog, **the** book

- A **demonstrative adjective** tells which one. *This, that, these,* and *those* can be used as demonstrative adjectives. Use *this* and *these* to talk about things that are nearby.
  This book is very interesting. I have read **that** book, too.
  Note: Never use *here* or *there* after the adjectives *this, that, these,* and *those*.

- A **proper adjective** is made from a proper noun. Capitalize proper adjectives.
  French bread

Adverbs

An **adverb** describes a verb, an adjective, or another adverb. Adverbs tell how, when, where, or to what extent.

- Many adverbs end in -*ly*.
  suddenly   **foolishly**

- Some adverbs do not end in -*ly*. These include *now, then, very, too, often, always, again, sometimes, soon, later, first, far, now,* and *fast*.

- Some adverbs tell *how*.
  He **quickly** shut the door.

- Some adverbs tell *when*.
  She may run **again**.

- Some adverbs tell *where*.
  She lived **abroad** for a year.

- Some adverbs tell *to what extent*.
  Alexis **narrowly** missed winning the election.

Prepositions

A preposition shows a relationship between a word in a sentence and a noun or pronoun that follows the preposition. Prepositions tell when, where, what kind, how, or how much.

- This is a list of some common prepositions:

about	behind	in	since
above	below	into	through
across	beside	like	to
after	between	near	toward
against	beyond	of	under
along	by	off	until
around	down	on	unto
at	for	over	up
before	from	past	with

Conjunctions

The words *and, or,* and *but* are **coordinating** conjunctions.

- **Coordinating** conjunctions may be used to join words within a sentence.
  She bought bread **and** milk.

- A comma and a coordinating conjunction can be used to join two or more simple sentences.

   The helicopter landed on the field, **and** a crowd gathered around it.

- A **subordinating** conjunction relates one clause to another. Dependent clauses begin with a subordinating conjunction. Subordinating conjunctions include *because, so, if, although, when, where, as, while, though, than, as if, whenever, since, wherever, after, often, over,* and *before.*

   When the roller coaster topped the first hill, I let out a wild scream.

Appositives

An **appositive** is a phrase that identifies a noun.

- Most **appositives** are separated from the rest of a sentence by commas. These appositives just give more information about the nouns they describe.

   Tara, **my friend who figure skates,** is traveling to Dallas.

- Some appositives should not be set off by commas. If an appositive is vital to the meaning of the sentence, it should not be set off by commas.

   My sister **Katie** likes to read on the porch.

Comparisons

- The **comparative form** of an adjective or an adverb compares two people, places, or things. The comparative form is often followed by "than." To compare two people, places, or things, add *-er* to short adjectives and adverbs.

   A giraffe is **taller** than an elephant.

- The **superlative form** of an adjective or an adverb compares three or more people, places, or things. The article *the* usually comes before the superlative form. To compare three or more items, add *-est* to short adjectives and adverbs.

   The giraffe is the **tallest** land animal.

- The word *more* is used with longer adjectives to compare two persons, places, or things. Use the word *most* to compare three or more persons, places, or things.

   Duane is **more excited** than Mario.
   Kiki is the **most excited** student of them all.

- Sometimes the words *good* and *bad* are used to compare. These words change forms in comparisons.

   Mario is a **good** athlete. Kiki is a **better** athlete.
   The basketball court is in **bad** shape. The tennis court is in **worse** shape than before.

Homophones

Homophones are words that sound alike but have different spellings and meanings.

- Common homophones:

are	**Are** is a form of the verb *be*.
our	**Our** is a possessive pronoun.
hour	An **hour** is sixty minutes.
its	**Its** is a possessive pronoun.
it's	**It's** is a contraction of the words *it is*.
there	**There** is an adverb meaning "in that place."
their	**Their** is a possessive pronoun.
they're	**They're** is a contraction made from the words *they are*.
two	**Two** is a number.
to	**To** can be a preposition meaning "toward." *To* can also be used with a verb to form an infinitive.
too	**Too** means "also." **Too** can mean "more than enough."
your	**Your** is a possessive pronoun.
you're	**You're** is a contraction made from the words *you are*.
whose	**Whose** is a possessive pronoun.
who's	**Who's** is a contraction made from the words *who* and *is* or *who* and *has*.
than	**Than** is a subordinating conjunction used to compare.
then	**Then** can be an adverb that tells about time. It can also mean "therefore."
principal	A **principal** is a person with authority.
principle	A **principle** is a general rule or code of behavior.
waist	The **waist** is the middle part of the body.
waste	To **waste** something is to use it in a careless way.
aloud	**Aloud** means out loud or able to be heard.
allowed	**Allowed** is a form of the verb *allow*.

Addressing Letters

The envelope below shows how to address a letter. A friendly letter and a business letter are addressed the same way.

Arthur Quinn
35 Rand St.
Chicago, IL 60606

Kim Lee
1555 Montague Blvd.
Memphis, TN 38106

Business Letters

A **business letter** is a formal letter. You would write a business letter to a company, an employer, a newspaper, or any person you do not know well. A business letter looks a lot like a friendly letter, but a business letter also includes the name and address of the business you are writing to. The **greeting** of a business letter begins with a capital letter and ends with a colon (:).